Books by Mildred Tengbom

Is Your God Big Enough?
The Bonus Years (reissued as *September Morning*)
Table Prayers
A Life to Cherish (reissued as *Devotions for New Mothers*)
Especially for Mother
No Greater Love: The Story of Clara Maass
Mealtime Prayers
Fill My Cup, Lord (co-authored with Luverne C. Tengbom)
Bible Readings for Families (co-authored with
  Luverne C. Tengbom)
Does Anyone Care How I Feel?
I Wish I Felt Good All the Time
Does It Make Any Difference What I Do?
Talking Together about Love and Sexuality
Sometimes I Hurt
Help for Bereaved Parents
Help for Families of the Terminally Ill
Bible Readings for Mothers
The Spirit of God Was Moving

Mildred Tengbom

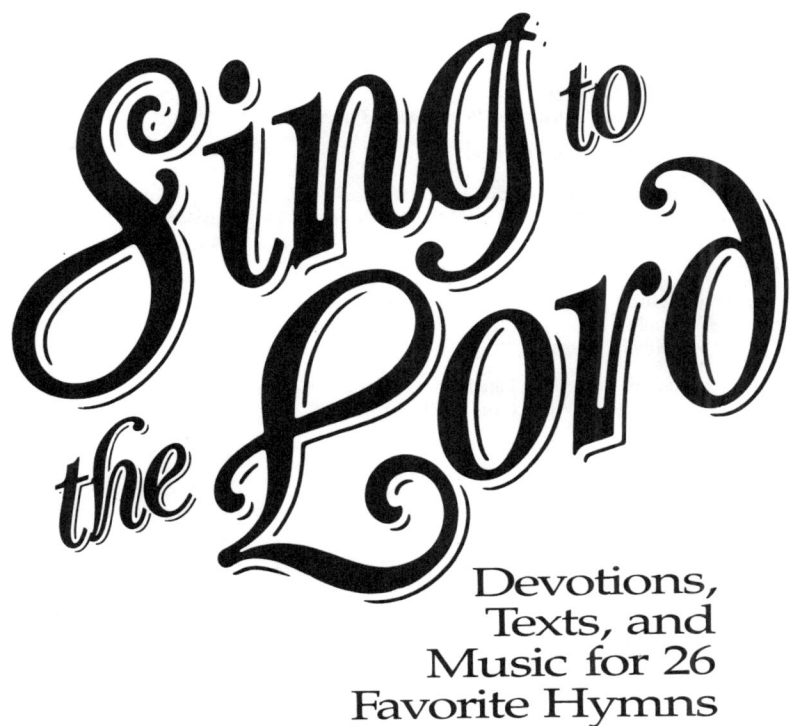

Sing to the Lord

Devotions, Texts, and Music for 26 Favorite Hymns

Augsburg • Minneapolis

SING TO THE LORD
Devotions, Texts, and Music for 26 Favorite Hymns

Copyright © 1988 Augsburg Fortress

All rights reserved. Except for brief quotations in critical articles or reviews, no part of this book may be reproduced in any manner without prior written permission from the publisher. Write to: Permissions, Augsburg Fortress, 426 S. Fifth St., Box 1209, Minneapolis MN 55440.

Scripture quotations unless otherwise noted are from the Holy Bible: New International Version. Copyright 1978 by the New York International Bible Society. Used by permission of Zondervan Bible Publishers.

Scripture quotations marked NAS are from the New American Standard Bible © The Lockman Foundation 1960, 1962, 1963, 1968, 1971, 1972, 1973, 1975. Used by permission.

Scripture quotations marked JB are from The Jerusalem Bible, copyright 1966 by Darton, Longman and Todd, Ltd. and Doubleday and Company. Used by permission of the publisher.

Some material in "The Meal We Eat Together," p. 147, is from *Visions of a World Hungry* by Thomas G. Pettepiece. Copyright © 1979 by The Upper Room and quoted in *A Guide to Prayer for Ministers and Other Servants* by Rueben Job and Norman Shawchuck. Copyright © 1983 by The Upper Room, 1908 Grand Ave., P.O. Box 189, Nashville, TN 37202. Used by permission of the publisher.

Library of Congress Cataloging-in-Publication Data

Tengbom, Mildred.
   Sing to the Lord : devotions, texts, and music for 26 favorite hymns / Mildred Tengbom.
     p. cm.
   ISBN 0-8066-2385-3
   1. Hymns—Devotional use. I. Title.
BV340.T46   1988
264'.2—dc19
                                                                                    88-39962
                                                                                       CIP

Manufactured in the U.S.A.   AF 10-5801
1 2 3 4 5 6 7 8 9 0 1 2 3 4 5 6 7 8 9

To two of my former book editors,
Roland Seboldt of Augsburg
and Jaroslav (Jary) Vajda of Concordia,
writers in their own rights, and musicians as well,
Roland as choirmaster and organist,
Jary as poet, hymn writer, and pianist,
I dedicate this book—a small, inadequate token of appreciation
for their years of encouraging me
not only in my writing ministry
but also on my journey of faith
with my Lord and Savior, Jesus Christ,
to whom I owe all.

Contents

O Little Town of Bethlehem	9
O God, Our Help in Ages Past	16
Jesus Calls Us; O'er the Tumult	23
Just as I Am, without One Plea	30
Love Divine, All Loves Excelling	37
A Mighty Fortress Is Our God	44
My Faith Looks Up to Thee	51
There's a Wideness in God's Mercy	58
The Lord's My Shepherd	65
Rock of Ages, Cleft for Me	72
Amazing Grace, How Sweet the Sound	79
O Love That Will Not Let Me Go	86
When Peace, like a River	93
In the Cross of Christ I Glory	100
I Know that My Redeemer Lives!	107
Praise to the Lord, the Almighty	114
Jesus, Savior, Pilot Me	121
What a Friend We Have in Jesus	128
For the Beauty of the Earth	135
The Church's One Foundation	142

O Master, Let Me Walk with You	149
God Moves in a Mysterious Way	156
He Leadeth Me: Oh, Blessed Thought!	163
Immortal, Invisible, God Only Wise	170
Take My Life, that I May Be	177
Now Thank We All Our God	184

Week 1

O Little Town of Bethlehem

Phillips Brooks, 1835–1893   Lewis H. Redner, 1831–1908

1. O little town of Bethlehem, How still we see thee lie!
   Above thy deep and dreamless sleep The silent stars go by;
   Yet in thy dark streets shineth The everlasting light.
   The hopes and fears of all the years Are met in thee tonight.

2. For Christ is born of Mary, And, gathered all above
   While mortals sleep, the angels keep Their watch of wond'ring love.
   O morning stars, together Proclaim the holy birth,
   And praises sing to God the king, And peace to all the earth!

3. How silently, how silently The wondrous gift is giv'n!
   So God imparts to human hearts The blessings of his heav'n.
   No ear may hear his coming; But, in this world of sin,
   Where meek souls will receive him, still The dear Christ enters in.

4. O holy Child of Bethlehem, Descend to us, we pray;
   Cast out our sin, and enter in, Be born in us today.
   We hear the Christmas angels The great glad tidings tell;
   Oh, come to us, abide with us, Our Lord Immanuel!

Day 1   Prov. 13:12   "O little town of Bethlehem."

What Do You Enjoy Most?

What can be a reliable guideline to follow if we are in that position in life where we can choose a vocation or an occupation? Or if that time is past for us, what word of wisdom can we pass on to those wondering what to do with their lives? Simply stated: do what brings you the most peace and joy, for usually that is what you will do best.

Phillips Brooks finally found his place as a preacher and writer after first trying unsuccessfully to be a teacher in a secular school. Harvard University and the Episcopal Theological Seminary at Alexandria, Virginia, prepared him for his pastoral ministry which culminated in 27 distinguished years at Trinity Church, Boston. Attracted by his preaching, the church grew. When he published his first volume of sermons, 200,000 people purchased them. Teaching at a seminary, and at Harvard and Yale further enlarged his ministry. His travels enhanced his sermons. He had visited Bethlehem before writing "O Little Town of Bethlehem."

Lewis Henry Redner, the composer of the melody for this hymn, found his place of lively pleasure in two areas. Highly successful in real estate, he became very wealthy. Wealth gave him leisure to pursue musical studies followed by filling positions as organist for four churches. Then he began to pour his energies into serving as superintendent, choir director, and organist for the Sunday school of the chapel of Holy Trinity Church in Philadelphia where Brooks was pastor before going to Boston. In 19 years Redner saw the Sunday school enrollment grow from 36 to over 1000. "Write a Christmas song for the children," Redner had begged Brooks in 1868. "I'll write the melody." And thus this lovely Christmas hymn came into being.

Fortunate indeed are we if we are in positions where we are doing the work we enjoy most. If we are not, we can compensate by doing in our free time that which brings joy. Redner found his niche in the Sunday school. If you haven't found yours, dream, think, pray about it—and then dare to venture out.

Thank you, Father, for the gift of work which brings so much meaning to life.

Day 2   Luke 2:1-7   "For Christ is born of Mary."

That First Christmas Night

Poets and hymn writers have described that memorable night as serene and peaceful. The night itself may have wrapped peaceful arms around the sleeping inhabitants of that crowded Judean town, but the night was anything but peaceful for the chief characters.

We can only speculate as we try to reconstruct the preceding day. Were Mary and Joseph traveling on the east side of the Jordan, the route that was warmer in the winter? If so, had they left Jericho in the morning? Why didn't they stop at Jerusalem? On the outskirts of Jerusalem lived dearly loved and trusted kinswoman Elizabeth to whom Mary had first confided her secret.

The distance between Jerusalem and Bethlehem is about five miles. Surely as they approached Jerusalem Mary must have been having contractions. First babies usually are 10, 12, 15 and even more hours on the way to being born after the first contractions begin. Why then the deliberate bypassing of a familiar, cozy home and experienced, loving hands and arms to help her through the painful hours of delivery? Why the insistence to press on to Bethlehem? Had a cut-off date for enrolling been set? With travel delayed after the baby was born, would this have made them late? Or did Mary, way back then, realize who her child was and why it was so significant that he be born in Bethlehem? And how did Mary feel when enroute to Bethlehem they passed the monument raised to mark Rachel's grave? Rachel, who had died in childbirth while on a journey. Did that tomb strike fear to her heart?

Then the arrival at the jam-packed town, the contractions steadily getting harder, the search for a place—any place—yielding nothing until at last a cow shelter was found. And then the birth. Was poor, bumbling Joseph the midwife? Or did the innkeeper's wife finally come?

Take some moments this Christmas to ponder the event that has become so familiar to us. Let it come alive for you. Sit in awe and wonder before it. Let it speak its own message to you, and utter your own prayer of thanksgiving and praise.

Day 3   Heb. 12:2   "And praises sing to God the king."

What Love Is This!

It wasn't the first time the stars had looked down in amazement at the goings on between heaven and earth. Centuries earlier they had winked at one another in amusement over old childless Abraham's astonishment when he heard God saying, "Abraham, do you see all those stars up there? Some day you're going to have more descendants than all those stars." The stars could smile, for they knew far better than those humans below how limitless was the power of their creative God.

But wonderful as that night had been, it didn't begin to compare with this awe-filled night as they looked down, not at the sleeping inhabitants of Bethlehem, but at a young woman and the man by her side who were not sleeping. And then there was one last cry of pain, one last mighty push, and then an exclamation of joy and relief from the young mother: "It's all over!"

"It's all over!" she cried, but the stars covered their faces in sorrow, because they knew in reality that a life of suffering had just begun. And so the astonishment of the stars knew no limits when they heard chanting—the most glorious, harmonious chanting! The stars uncovered their eyes to look and were almost blinded by the brilliant light enveloping a huge, angelic choir. "Glory to God," the choir sang. Glory to God? God facing his own suffering and the suffering of his only, dearly loved Son and yet celebrating with joy? Celebrating with song the prospect of suffering? "And peace to his people on earth," the choir continued. Stunned, the stars struggled to comprehend the incomprehensible: God so loved those often unlovely earthdwellers below that he could only rejoice at the thought that the loving, intimate relationship he longed to have with them he soon would know more perfectly—even if it meant he must suffer!

Should not God's eagerness for deeper communion with us tug at our hearts until we give diligence and discipline to enter into a closer, more personal relationship with him? Why not schedule time each day for prayer to know God better?

Lord Jesus, your boundless love for me brings praise I hardly can express. Draw me near to you and help me love you fully.

Day 4   Luke 2:13-19   "Proclaim the holy birth."

How God Fills the Voids

The year was 1957. The place was Africa. My husband had just brought me and our wee baby daughter home from the hospital. "I wish our families could be here and see our baby!" I said.

That evening, as we were finishing our evening meal, we heard singing. "Who? What?" we asked each other and opened the door to look out. There stood our African friends. Song after song they sang. "It's our custom," one of them whispered. "When a baby is born, we go to the home and sing in celebration."

The young women in Mary's day observed the same custom. When the news of a birth ran through the village, the women sped to the house to encircle it and dance and sing.

Knowing about that custom led me to ask my husband a question when we were visiting Bethlehem. "How large is a host?" I asked.

"A very great number," he answered. "I don't think we can define it specifically. Why?"

I hesitated. "I was just noticing," I said, "the position of what is thought to be the shepherd's field and the possible location of the place where Jesus was born. And I've been wondering . . . if the shepherds heard the host of angels, maybe . . . couldn't it have been possible that Mary did too?" I was thinking of Mary so far from home, all alone with no one except Joseph to share her joy and her wistful wishing that her friends could be there to sing for her. Did God, understanding and caring, send a whole angelic choir to take their place? And later shepherds?

Speculation, some will say. Yes. But it is no speculation that God knows our every circumstance and cares about us and that he is gentle and kind. This assurance can bring special cheer to us during times of loneliness and separation from loved ones. "I wish they were here with me," we say. When they can't be, let us ask God to open our eyes to see those he's sending to take their place. They may appear a bit disguised, but if we look carefully, eventually we'll distinguish them.

For all you've sent into my life at various times to fill the holes left by the absence of my loved ones, I give you thanks, O Lord.

Day 5   Eccl. 4:6   "How silently, how silently."

Gifts Silently Given

Many Christmas hymns refer to the peacefulness of that night that shines like a brilliant meteor in contrast to all other nights the centuries have ever known. "Silent night." "The world in solemn stillness lay." "Earth was hushed and still."

Why all this emphasis on quietness and peacefulness and being hushed and stilled? Does not this line give us a clue: "How silently, how silently, the wondrous gift is given"?

How many of the gifts God gives us are accompanied by silence. Dawn silently parts the lids of morning. The stars and the moon quietly turn on their lights at night. Dew softly settles on thirsty foliage, keeping the desert alive. Trees, grass, flowers, and crops grow noiselessly—at least the human ear cannot hear them grow. Babies grow silently, hidden within their mothers. We see the movements from their hiccups but cannot hear them. The deepest love between humans is often expressed wordlessly. The forgiveness of God frequently is experienced silently. Other gifts of grace steal into our hearts: hope, courage, perseverance, determination to carry on. And, as the writer of this hymn stated, "No ear may hear his coming, but in this world of sin, where meek souls will receive him still, the dear Christ enters in."

How will it be for us in the coming Christmas? Will all the hustle, bustle, jostling, pushing, snapping, crying, and worrying that too often characterize our Christmas preparations rob us of the quietness we need to receive Christ and the gifts of the Spirit he wishes to give us? When will we who call ourselves by the Christ child's name learn to cast aside and be done with some of this world's crazy, commercial customs and learn to be still, so that "silently, silently, God's wondrous gift" can come to us more freshly and more fully than ever. Maybe this year we can make a beginning by centering more time each day, both for ourselves and our families, around worship of Jesus whom we truly love.

We want to celebrate Christmas, Lord, because your coming has meant so much to us. Help us to break loose from the frantic, materialistic pattern the world has dictated to us.

Day 6   Matt. 1:1-16   "Cast out our sin and enter in."

What Does Jesus' Genealogy Mean?

Years ago Norman Rockwell in his symbolic sketch of a family tree included not only Yankees and Confederates but yeomen and buccaneers, preachers and pioneers, puritans and aristocrats, and people from many ethnic backgrounds.

As we look at the genealogy of Jesus given us by Matthew, we note two remarkable things: the absence of the names of Sarah, Rebecca, and Rachel, and the inclusion of Tamar, Ruth, Rahab, and Bathsheba. By Old Testament standards Sarah, Rebecca, and Rachel were righteous, God-fearing women. The others? Tamar disguised herself as a prostitute and lured her father-in-law into an illicit sexual relationship with her. Ruth was a noble woman but was considered by the Jews to be a foreigner, not one of the covenant people. Rahab, we think, made her living as a prostitute. Bathsheba's name is not mentioned; instead, Matthew refers to her as "Uriah's wife," underscoring her adulterous relationship to David.

How can we account for the fact that God not only allowed three disreputable women and one foreigner to be included in the lineage of Jesus but that their names also are boldly recorded for all generations to read?

Jesus himself by his actions repeatedly gave the answer. He chose to stay with Zacchaeus, who had misused public funds. He allowed a former prostitute to bathe his feet with her tears—and in public. He went to a feast put on by the crooked tax collectors. And finally he summed it all up by saying, "I have not come to call the righteous, but sinners" (Mark 2:17). In other words, if he was going to call them, he had to be with them, getting to know them, and they had to learn to know him.

At Christmas and Easter, especially, people flock to church. This Christmas why not take advantage of that openness of spirit and invite some whose manner of life you have criticized? Let Jesus call them through you. And don't stop with the Christmas celebrations, either. Follow through, and see God do a miracle.

Forgive me, Lord, when I've thought or acted like a self-righteous Pharisee. Help me see others as I want you to see me, a sinner yes, but a sinner saved by your grace.

Week 2

O God, Our Help in Ages Past

Isaac Watts, 1674–1748, alt.   William Croft, 1678–1727

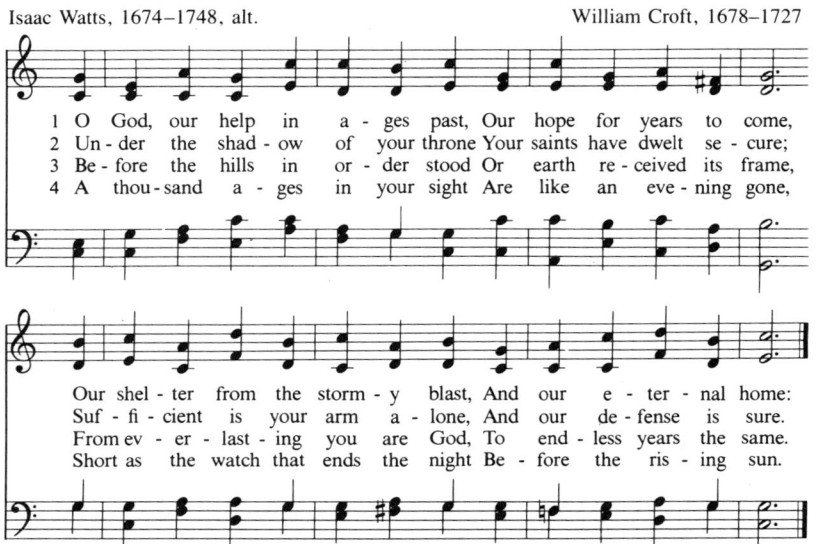

1. O God, our help in ages past, Our hope for years to come, Our shelter from the stormy blast, And our eternal home:
2. Under the shadow of your throne Your saints have dwelt secure; Sufficient is your arm alone, And our defense is sure.
3. Before the hills in order stood Or earth received its frame, From everlasting you are God, To endless years the same.
4. A thousand ages in your sight Are like an evening gone, Short as the watch that ends the night Before the rising sun.

5. Time, like an ever-rolling stream,
   Soon bears us all away;
   We fly forgotten, as a dream
   Dies at the op'ning day.

6. O God, our help in ages past,
   Our hope for years to come,
   Still be our guard while troubles last
   And our eternal home!

Day 1   Phil. 4:11-13   "O God, our help."

Accepting Challenges

Isaac Watts early learned to meet life's hardships and challenges with courage, conviction, and action. His grandfather, a naval commander of a Dutch ship, ordered the ship he was on blown to bits rather than have the enemy do it. His father, a Nonconformist deacon in the state church, went to prison for his beliefs. When Watts's father was imprisoned a second time, his mother sent nine-year-old Watts to live with a pastor friend. Watts took advantage of the opportunity to learn Greek, Hebrew, Latin, and French from his guardian. Years later a wealthy physician offered to educate Watts in a state university. Watts declined. "Thoughts should be as free as wind," he said, and chose instead to enter a Nonconformist academy. A young woman spurned his proposal of marriage. Watts refused to let that sour him. After the woman died, Watts published her literary efforts. Also, when he was deprived of a home, he compensated by tutoring children.

He did not let his five-foot stature deter him from entering the pulpit. He was determined to take advantage of his rich voice and concentrate on developing rich rhetoric and meeting the needs of the people. His congregation grew. When ill health forced him from the pulpit he accepted the invitation of a good friend, Sir Thomas Abney, to stay in his home. To that home came the educated and elite of the day, providing intellectual stimuli for Watts's ever-creative and inquiring mind. Watts had been highly critical of the clumsily paraphrased and unsingable psalms used in the churches. Galled by his criticism, someone exclaimed, "Well, then give us something better!" Watts proceeded to do just that and wrote over 600 hymns, many acknowledged to be some of the finest in the English language and are still sung today.

We too may find ourselves critical of the way something is being done or isn't being done in our church or churches. If we can respond as effectively as Watts, well and good! But if all we can do is complain and criticize, let's shut up and lend support instead.

Gracious God, teach me to contribute, not to criticize, and to enrich and not tear down.

Day 2   Phil. 2:4   "O God, our help."

Giving Love in Desert Places

The TV evening news told the story of a courageous, wise woman who, divorced by her husband many years ago and left with three small children to raise, found help against bitterness and despair in a way few would think of finding it.

Living on the border of Mexico, she happened one day to drive past the garbage dumps of Juarez and was appalled by the shanty town she saw and the women and children scrounging around for food. Unable to forget them, she began to collect leftover food from the hospital where she worked as a nurses' aide. Weekends, enlisting the help of her children, she cooked huge kettles of food in her kitchen and brought them to the dump. Next she coaxed business people into providing a small building that could serve as kitchen and clinic and cajoled doctors into volunteering to treat the ill there. She took on a second job in order to buy shoes for the children of the dump. She continued this until her hair whitened and her strength waned. But through her years of service help had come to her personally as she had been able to see the suffering Christ in the faces of the poor of the garbage dump.

Some, instead of responding to loss as this selfless single mother did, react and lash out in anger. They focus on their own loss, their own feelings. As they continue to concentrate on self and the injustice they feel God and life have dealt them, they begin to collide with others. If they do not dare do this in their business associations, subtly or otherwise, at home they push others down instead of helping them. They refuse the help God offers them. The marginal note for Psalm 46:1 in the New American Standard Bible reads: "God is abundantly available for help in tight places." The Texan single mother, in her tight place, found that abundantly available help as she gave herself to those whose need was even greater than her own. Her course of action brought life and joy both to herself and others. The choice is ours. How will we respond to the help God offers us?

Give to us, O God, from whom all good counsel comes, wisdom to respond gratefully to the help you make available to us.

Day 3   Psalm 42   "Our help in ages past."

Remember!

Martha pounded the wall. "Why us?" she shouted. "Why us?"

"Martha." Her husband's calm voice swung her around.

"We've no choices left!" Martha flared.

"Wrong! We don't have many choices, but we do have two. We can let this sorrow that has come to us embitter and poison us, or we can let it purify us."

Martha crumbled sobbing to the floor by her husband's bed and buried her face in the blankets. Four years had passed since her husband's doctor had said, "I'm so sorry. Cancer. We'll try to hold it in remission." They had succeeded until now. Forewarned, they had taken care of all business affairs. They had gone on dreamed-of camping trips with their children. Involvement in Bible classes and small groups had enriched their lives. God had never been more present and friends more supportive. All this Martha now remembered. Her sobs subsided. If God not only had seen them through the past four difficult years but had sprinkled the years with laughter, love, and hope, couldn't she trust him for the future also? "I'm sorry," she said, lifting her tear-wet face. "It's just that sometimes it gets so hard, and I'm so human."

Remember, remember, remember! The word echoes and re-echoes throughout the Old and New Testaments. "God remembered Noah," "God remembered Abraham," and "God remembered Rachel" we read. Because God has remembered us, David said, we should "give thanks to the Lord," we should remember the wonders he has done.

When the future looks forbidding and hope burns feebly, pause and remember all the goodness of God toward you in the past. Make it a daily practice to remember something new for which to thank him. And watch. As you do, he who has been your help in the past will assure you that you may confidently put your hope in him for the future also.

Grant, O Father, that instead of brooding over my sorrows and troubles I may busy myself in recalling your goodness to me.

Day 4   Eccl. 3:1-15   "Before the hills in order stood."

What If God Was Not Orderly?

Daily the universe blesses us with orderliness. Our earth home rotates around the sun always at a distance of about 93 million miles. If the earth moved closer, it would spell disaster for us. Also because of this orderliness of the universe, our lives can be divided between the needed cycles of wakefulness and sleep, work, and rest. Larger cycles mark our lives too. Spring follows winter; summer comes on the heels of spring; autumn brings coolness and harvest; and winter spells a change of activity for most humans and rest for the earth. In the sky above us Mercury, Venus, Mars, Jupiter, Saturn, Uranus, Neptune, Pluto, and about 100,000 observable minor stars and their satellites rotate in their courses. Only this assured orderliness makes moon landings possible. Only this orderliness makes future space exploration possible. Clearly our Creator God is a God of order.

Paul emphasized the need for order in worship when he wrote to the exuberant Christians in Corinth about how they should conduct services that included speaking in tongues. "Do not forbid speaking in tongues," he wrote, "but everything should be done in a fitting and orderly way" (1 Cor. 14:39-40).

Orderliness in daily life can help ensure calmness and relief from some tensions. We never lose out when we follow the old adage, "A place for everything, and everything in its place." An ordered daily routine—a time to get up, to eat, to leave for school, to do assigned chores, and finally go to bed—all this can bring a sense of security to children growing up. "There is a time for everything and a season for every activity under heaven," the philosopher of Ecclesiastes wrote. A time yes, and a place. Put the two together and receive the gift of order.

Dear Lord, let our ordered lives reflect the beauty of your orderly universe.

Day 5   Matt. 22:31-33   "We fly forgotten."

Never Forgotten

Easter Sunday afternoon, 1985, during our year and one-half sojourn in Singapore, we went exploring the lovely garden island. Our drive to the northern end of the island led us to an isolated, undeveloped area shared by the city dump and cemeteries. The burial grounds of the different religious faiths lay adjacent to each other. The Bahai area looked like a military cemetery with its severely simple grey headstones. The Moslem and Christian areas sheltered the usual multi-shaped, multi-colored monuments. The Chinese cemetery, which stretched for miles, housed elaborate memorial structures, shaped somewhat like old fainting couches without legs. Colored pictures and scenes engraved on the tiles adorned the front ends and sometimes a picture of the deceased was enclosed under glass. As we drove along, the road narrowed. We bumped over potholes until we came to the Hindu cemetery. Here we saw few monuments, only simple markers.

What motivates all humans to want to mark their place of burial? I wondered that day. Is it not a desire to be remembered? Even though most of us know that after death we shall be remembered by only the generations that have known us, still we want our names and dates of birth and death recorded in enduring stone.

Most meaningful and comforting for us as Christians, however, is the knowledge that we are engraved, not on stone, but on the palms of God's hands (Isa. 49:16). In the verses previous we read Zion had been worrying that the Lord had forgotten his people. God chides Zion and asks if a mother can forget her baby nursing at her breast. So close are you to me, God declares, that I will never forget you.

Yes, time, like an ever-rolling stream will one day bear us all away. But while in the memories of others we may "fly forgotten, as a dream dies at the op'ning day," we shall never be forgotten by God.

Faithful, loving God, we thank you that though years after we die perhaps no one will remember us, still you will never forget us but that after death you will take us to be with you.

Day 6   Psalm 90   "Ages past . . . our shelter . . . years to come."

What Age Do You Live In?

Neurological and psychiatric researchers temporarily blotted out time for six volunteers. Because they could not remember the past, life lost its meaning. Because they could not remember the present, they withdrew and became depressed. Because they had no sense of there being a future, anxiety and fear disappeared, as did hope and motivation.

Isaac Watts refers to all three periods of time in this hymn: "O God, our help in ages past," "our [present] shelter from the stormy blast," and "our hope for years to come."

Awareness of being part of the past, among other things, can bring us courage and call us to struggle to be and do more than we otherwise would. Helen Keller referred to this. "When your thoughts become pessimistic, when it seems as if all are deafened by self-interest and greed," she said, "turn the pages of your history book. It is filled with heroes and martyrs who joyfully pushed aside ambition and gave their lives to God's service. The world needs more of this spirit. Many a desert place remains where the sun of love and the light of truth have not shone."

But we must not get stuck in the past, as we may be tempted to do as we get older. As strength wanes, our hope in the eternal home God has promised us needs to become ever more robust.

But we must not get stuck in the future, either. Nelson Trout, a pastor, tells of how his little son kept asking, "When is Santa Claus coming?" "Tomorrow he'll be here," his father kept answering. On Christmas morning the little fellow woke up and walked into the living room and saw all the packages under the tree. "Daddy," he screamed, "it's tomorrow!"

Times past, times present, times to come. As we live in all three we will find purpose for living, enthusiasm, a yearning to be sociable and to reach out to others, motivation to keep living as long as we're living, and bright shining hope for the future. Let's not lose out on any of these good gifts by getting locked into any one period of time.

Lord of all times, teach me to keep in balance times past, times present, and times to come, and to live in all three.

Week 3

Jesus Calls Us; O'er the Tumult

Cecil F. Alexander, 1823–1895
William H. Jude, 1851–1922

1. Jesus calls us; o'er the tumult Of our life's wild, restless sea, Day by day his clear voice sounding, Saying, "Christian, follow me."
2. As of old St. Andrew heard it By the Galilean lake, Turned from home and toil and kindred, Leaving all for his dear sake.
3. Jesus calls us from the worship Of the vain world's golden store, From each idol that would keep us, Saying, "Christian, love me more."
4. In our joys and in our sorrows, Days of toil and hours of ease, Still he calls, in cares and pleasures, "Christian, love me more than these."

5. Jesus calls us! In your mercy,
    Savior, make us hear your call,
    Give our hearts to your obedience,
    Serve and love you best of all.

Day 1   Matt. 4:18-20   "His clear voice sounding."

When Nobodys Become Somebodys

"Today I became a person in anthropology class!" our 15-year-old announced joyously one day when she came home. "I'm a person in science and English too, but not in math yet."

"What do you mean?" I asked.

"Well," she said, setting her books on the counter, "today the anthropology teacher called me by name."

So intimate is God's relationship with us that he sees us as persons, not just as part of the crowd. When we read the Gospels we note how Jesus called the disciples one by one. Hagar, the surrogate mother, who was cast aside because she was no longer needed, was in the desert dying of thirst and heard God calling.

Cecil Frances Alexander, the author of this hymn, also heard Christ's call. Answering that call meant establishing a school for the deaf with the help of her sister. After her marriage to the archbishop and primate of Ireland, it meant sore, blistered feet as she walked miles to care for the sick and bring food to the poor. She loved children and wrote hymns for them. She pleaded with adults not to misjudge children's ability to grasp even profound truths. "Let us teach them the Creed," she begged, "and let us not be afraid of using complex words."

Hearing and responding to God's call metamorphosed the lives of the disciples and Cecil Alexander and brought hope to Hagar. Are your circumstances tossing you around like a paper boat far out at sea? Are strength and courage failing? Are opportunities for advancement luring you which, however, would mean sacrificing integrity? Do you wonder if God has anything for you to do? Do friends or family cast you aside? Do you wonder if God really cares about you? The psalmist did. "When I consider your heavens . . . the moon and the stars . . . what is man that you are mindful of him?" he asked (Ps. 8:3-4).

The disciples, Hagar, and Cecil Alexander discovered that God knows and cares about us. We are "somebodys" to God. So put your name in place of Hagar's and hear God asking, "[your name], what troubles you? Fear not. Only follow me."

Day 2 John 1:29-42   "St. Andrew heard it."

Just Andrew

People often refer to brothers, sisters, or children of famous people as "so-and-so's brother." So it was for Andrew. He was Peter's brother. "Quiet, unassuming guy," people said. Quiet, yes, but not inactive. Not Andrew. As soon as John the Baptist called his attention to Jesus, Andrew hurried off to find Peter. Andrew believed important finds should be shared.

Andrew cared. When the stomachs of people listening to Jesus began to growl because of hunger, Andrew looked around for food. He brought what he found to Jesus, five loaves and two fishes, though possibly he wondered how these could feed so many.

When the Greeks came asking to see Jesus, Andrew was the one who relayed the message to Jesus. Andrew's circle of concern grew ever wider: first his own brother, then his hungry fellow Jews, and finally the Greeks. Little did he guess the results would be like the short waves of radio reaching out thousands of miles. Peter assumed a prominent position of leadership in the church. Many of the Jews formed the first church, and the Greeks became the first fruits of a world church.

And Andrew? Andrew was quite content to be just Andrew. Not one of the Big Three—Peter, James, and John—but just Andrew.

What peace comes to all of us as we accept ourselves just as we are without wishing we were someone else whom we admire greatly. This means accepting our personality traits. Has God given us the ability to care about people? To cross cultures? To enter into the hurts of others? Accepting ourselves also means being grateful for and using faithfully whatever our gifts are, whether they be to maintain church buildings, clean church kitchens, teach Sunday school, be foster parents, or whatever. Or maybe we, like Andrew, have our own quiet way of witnessing to Jesus or bringing people to church. Maybe ours is the gift of calling attention to available resources when either our church or people wonder how they are going to meet certain needs. Will we let Andrew teach us that God values us just as we are and so we can be content?

O Christ, help me to rejoice in being just me.

Day 3 Hos. 13:4-8; 14:1-17 "The vain world's golden store."

Home by Way of the Wilderness

He sat holding his head in his hands. He had worked so hard to excel in real estate and had succeeded beyond his most extravagant dreams. He had moved his family into a luxurious new home, had given them everything they had asked—and more—and now the unbelievable had happened: the police had locked up his son for drug trafficking. His little universe was spinning crazily out of orbit, and his head was spinning with it.

Lawyers' and psychiatrists' fees gobbled up his savings and forced him to sell his home. Emotionally spent, he had no energy left to sell houses, so he took a routine job as janitor of a large apartment unit. His wife, angry and frustrated, divorced him. Then finally, finally, he found his way home to God.

"When the things on which we have rested our hopes turn out to be incapable of delivering the goods we had hoped for," Joseph Sittler writes in *Grace Notes and Other Fragments* (Fortress Press), "this is grace by way of judgment; it is education by way of disappointment, and illumination by way of darkness. In the Old Testament God led the people home by way of the wilderness. That may not be the most comfortable way to go home, but it may sometimes be the only way."

Do you now find yourself in the wilderness with the sun burning and the stones underfoot hurting as you walk and stumble and fall and get up to stagger along again? Or are some of your loved ones wandering in the wilderness? Don't give up hope. God had words of encouragement for the wilderness journey too: "But if from there [after you have forsaken following gods that cannot help] you seek the Lord your God, you will find him if you look for him with all your heart and with all your soul. When you are in distress and all these things have happened to you, then in later days you will return to the Lord your God and obey him. For the Lord your God is a merciful God; he will not abandon or destroy you" (Deut. 4:29-31).

Walk beside us and see us through the wilderness, faithful God of Moses, Miriam, and Aaron.

Day 4   Psalm 5   "In our sorrows."

Sorrow's Gentle Benediction

The day before had been one of life's saddest for King David as he had stumbled barefoot over the rocky trail away from Jerusalem with covered head, "weeping as he went."

A long line of tragedies had preceded this awful day. First he, middle-aged David, had lusted after the wife of another, seduced her, made her pregnant, and then arranged for her husband to be murdered to cover up his sin.

But God loved David, and so he sent the prophet Nathan to David. David had repented, but the child who was born died.

Then, like father, like son, David's sons began to misbehave. Amon lusted after his half-sister, Tamar, raped her, and then despised her. Tamar's brother, Absalom, in rage, killed Amon, and then fled. David grieved over his son Amon's death, and his son Absalom's sin, so when later Absalom feigned repentance, David accepted him with a kiss. But Absalom knew no genuine repentance; he stole the hearts of the people, and sent his father fleeing.

The night of his flight David lay down exhausted, grief for his sons ripping open his heart, remorse and regret over his former sin searing his soul, and anxiety for his safety and his future distressing him. Yet out of the nettle of danger, distress, and grief, David was able to pluck the flower of peace. "The Lord sustains me," he said simply (Ps. 3:5).

No matter in what form tragedy, grief, or sorrow may visit us, as we cry to God in utter helplessness he will garrison our hearts with peace. Bishop Herbert Chilstrom of the Evangelical Lutheran Church in America expressed it this way after some months had passed following his son's suicide. "The happiest, sweetest, tenderest homes are not those where there has been no sorrow, but those which have been overshadowed with grief, and where Christ's comfort was accepted. The very memory of the sorrow is a gentle benediction that broods over the household, like the silence that comes after prayer. There is a blessing from God in every burden of sorrow."

Bless me with your benediction, compassionate God.

Day 5   Hosea 4   "Savior, make us hear your call."

Jungles Can Become Gardens

Adulterer. Alcoholic. Murderer. The whispered accusations drove Svidrigailov, one of the chief characters in Dostoyevski's novel, *Crime and Punishment*, to flee his small town. That and boredom. It was the boredom that finally had galled him into murdering his wife whom he had married merely because she, with her wealth, could bail him out of jail. Scoundrel though he was, God still called out to Svidrigailov. How? Through softening his heart when he saw children with legs like pretzel sticks clinging to the ragged skirts of their harried mothers, either widows or wives of no-good men. Svidrigailov responded generously by giving the wealth that had become his when his wife died. But there the response ended. In the end he put a bullet to his head.

Rodion, Dostoyevski's other main character, also hid within his heart, as Carlo Carreto has expressed it, "a jungle of violence." Pride, frustrated ambitions, self-pity, moroseness, self-centeredness, and finally massive self-deception led this young student to murder a woman. But in the end Rodion was converted to Christ. What made the difference? What will make the difference for us and our loved ones? How can our jungles become dwelling places of peace?

The transformation won't come cheap. First, Christ's death was necessary. We also are reliant on God calling us. He calls in many and varied ways.

We also need the prayers and love of others. The unfaltering, long-suffering, unselfish love and prayers of a mother, sister, friend, and sweetheart encircled Rodion. Svidrigailov had no one to love him. We all need someone who will love us forever, but that love, too, is costly for those who love us.

And finally Rodion himself had to choose to respond affirmatively to God's call. What that would cost him Rodion learned in the weeks, months, and years that followed. Who wants bulldozers rearranging one's life? Yet without it, jungles of violence cannot become gardens of peace.

Be my gardener and the gardener of my loved ones, O God.

Day 6   Luke 19:1-10   "Give our hearts to your obedience."

The Meeting Behind Closed Doors

Goodness! Zacchaeus hadn't thought anyone would see him up there! Wasn't that why he had run on ahead and chosen a sycamore tree to climb into? The sycamore tree had low branches over which he could swing his leg and then hoist himself up farther until the heart-shaped, downy leaves that grew so luxuriantly would shut him out of view from those below, but he'd still be able to see the great rabbi. How astonished he was when Jesus stopped under the tree and looked up right at him!

"Come down, Zacchaeus. I need a place to stay tonight."

Stay with *him*? Unbelievable! At that time tax collectors weren't any more popular than IRS auditors are today. Less, in fact. People grumbled about how tax collectors drove Mercedeses and BMWs while other people rode bicycles, so to speak.

Once they got home, it took guts for Zacchaeus to let Jesus take him into a room alone and shut the door. At least we assume something like this happened, though we have no actual record. The evening news reporter was not allowed in. When the questioning began I wonder if at first Zacchaeus tried to offer excuses. "But, Jesus, everybody does it. You know that. You can't expect to do business these days without lying a little. What if I tampered with the records? Used some of the money for myself? I'm not the only one." As the questioning wore on did a perspiring Zacchaeus stammer, "Well, sure, I made a mistake or two, Jesus. But now that I've admitted it, won't you let me get back to my business?"

I really don't know if this is what actually happened behind those closed doors, nor does anyone else. All we know is eventually Zacchaeus must have come clean, for the next day and the next and the next Zacchaeus was busy, we might say, visiting charitable organizations and writing out checks and dictating letters to all he had cheated. And as Zacchaeus sought to make right where he had wronged, Jesus said, "Today has salvation come to your house!"

May my meeting with you, O lovely Jesus, lead me to true repentance.

Week 4

Just as I Am, without One Plea

Charlotte Elliott, 1789–1871
William B. Bradbury, 1816–1868

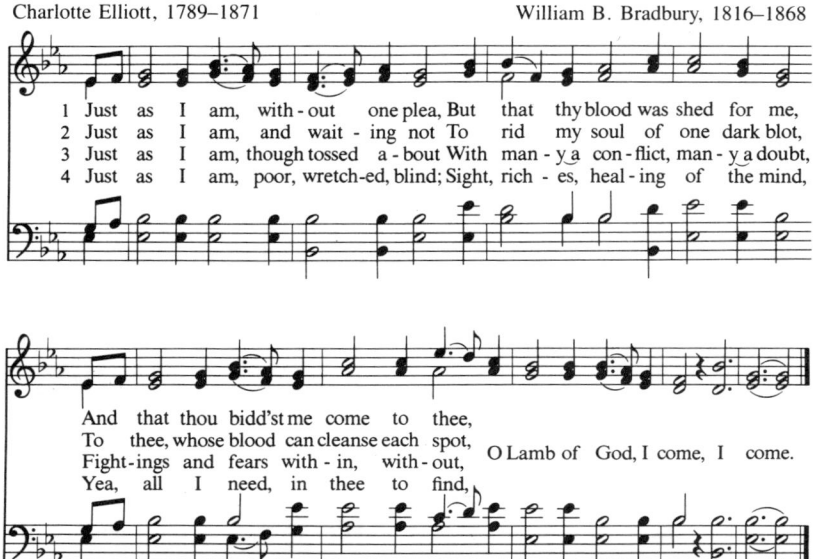

1 Just as I am, with-out one plea, But that thy blood was shed for me,
2 Just as I am, and wait-ing not To rid my soul of one dark blot,
3 Just as I am, though tossed a-bout With man-y a con-flict, man-y a doubt,
4 Just as I am, poor, wretch-ed, blind; Sight, rich-es, heal-ing of the mind,

And that thou bidd'st me come to thee,
To thee, whose blood can cleanse each spot,
Fight-ings and fears with-in, with-out,
Yea, all I need, in thee to find,

O Lamb of God, I come, I come.

5 Just as I am, thou wilt receive,
Wilt welcome, pardon, cleanse, relieve;
Because thy promise I believe,
O Lamb of God, I come, I come.

6 Just as I am; thy love unknown
Has broken ev'ry barrier down;
Now to be thine, yea, thine alone,
O Lamb of God, I come, I come.

Day 1   Isa. 55:1   "Just as I am . . . I come."

Call to Commitment

Life brimmed with promise for Charlotte Elliott. Her fame as a portrait artist and writer of humorous verse was spreading. Then tragedy struck. Charlotte's 30th birthday found her lying in bed, facing the prospect of being an invalid for life. "I'm no good for anything any more," she sobbed.

In her hour of need God brought to her bedside a well-known, penwise evangelist, Dr. Caesar Malan. "Come to Jesus just as you are," he pleaded, "with all your sins, fears, and conflicts." Charlotte did, and her life was turned around.

The good news of the gospel is that Jesus invites us to come just as we are. "Come," God invites, "though your sins are like scarlet, they shall be as white as snow." We don't have to wait, trying to do our own laundering and bleaching before we come.

But we have to come. As long as we remain uncommitted, hesitancy makes us ineffective. When Charlotte came, she saw things begin to happen. Hope replaced despair. Courage took over in place of fear. Her mind and pen began to craft hymns. One day her family attended a bazaar held to raise money to build a college for daughters of poor clergymen. Charlotte could not go, but alone at home she wrote, "Just as I am." Royalties from that hymn exceeded all the income from the charity bazaar. Over 1,000 people from all over the world wrote telling her how much the hymn had meant to them. The hymn has been sung hundreds of times as people have been invited to indicate their commitment by coming forward at the end of a meeting. At a Billy Graham campaign in Singapore, 20 in one particular area responded to the hymn. From those 20, 10 formed the nucleus of a congregation that five years later numbered 400. What if Charlotte Elliott had not come? What if she had not written the hymn? What if the 10 had not come?

Have we come? If we have, are we inviting others to come? Someone has said that God's favorite word is *come*. Knowing that and knowing all that can result after people have come to Jesus, should we not be encouraged to more often say to others, "Come. Come, just as you are, but come."

Teach me to love as you love, O Christ, and to say, "Come!"

Day 2   Matt. 26:36-46   "With many a conflict."

Two Feet Can Walk Only One Path

In the Garden of Gethsemane Jesus knew the Father's will for him was to pick up the sins of the world and bear them. Everything in him protested this. If he hadn't been so sure what the Father's will for him was, his struggle wouldn't have been so intense and painful. But he *knew,* and he didn't want to do it.

Our struggle to do God's will cannot assume the proportions nor the importance Christ's did, for the consequences of his obedience affected all peoples throughout all ages. But still our struggles remain our struggles, and they are never easy because doing God's will always runs counter to our own wills. We love God. We don't want to turn our backs on him completely, but we don't want to follow him unreservedly either.

"Why are you cheating on the hours you work?" God may ask us. "You know cheating is not being honest, and only by being honest can you honor the One who is truth."

Or, "Why do you feel you have to get even with someone who has mistreated you? Why can't you bear it silently? I did."

Or, "Why do you find it so hard to give me more than 60 seconds of worship a day when I give you 24 hours of life?"

Or, "How long are you going to continue not forgiving nor speaking to someone whom you think has offended you?"

If we are having a hard time obeying God, chances are it isn't because we don't know what he wants us to do, but because we don't want to do it. How good it is that we can bring this conflict to Jesus also. We can come just as we are with all our rebellion and unwillingness and ask him to give us the will to obey.

Gracious God, work in my heart true repentance, the repentance that grieves because of the harm and hurt I have caused you by my words and actions. Help me also to look forward to the better person I will become as I leave behind those unhealthy, crippling sins of which you have convicted me.

Day 3   Phil. 4:7-8   "Healing of the mind."

Healing of Memories

Julie couldn't understand why she felt so heavy in her spirit. When the heaviness increased, she went to her pastor. "Let us ask God to show you why you feel this way," he said.

After a week Julie went back to her pastor. "Well?" he asked. "All I could think about was my father," Julie said. Her pastor waited. Unexpectedly Julie began to sob. Still her pastor waited. Finally the words came jerking out. "He molested me—even when I was little. I hate him!"

Once again the two prayed. This time Julie poured out her feelings of anger and hatred. She wept. She asked God for forgiveness. Her pastor assured her she was. Julie's heaviness began to lift. "In the end, I almost flew home," she said.

The next time her parents visited her, Julie lovingly confronted her father, then told him she had forgiven him. He was silent. On subsequent visits she talked no more about the past, but continued expressing her love for him in whatever way she could. Finally the day came when he too wept and prayed, and Julie knew healing of the mind and memories had come to both of them.

Are there painful memories of the past that keep surfacing for you from time to time, making you feel unhappy? Maybe you think about them before you go to sleep at night. Or in church on Sunday when you are quiet for a few moments. Often those memories are connected with someone who has wronged you or it could be that you have wronged someone. If this is so, the first step toward healing will come with your confession, followed by the assurance that you are forgiven. We read in Isa. 43:25: "I, even I, am he who blots out your transgressions, for my own sake, and remembers your sins no more." Because of this God counsels us to "forget the former things" and not to dwell on the past (Isa. 43:18). "See," he says, "I am doing a new thing." This new thing for us could be a new, healthy relationship and the healing of half-forgotten but dark memories.

Dear Jesus, help me to bring to you what troubles me.

Day 4　　Luke 9:11　　　　　　　　　　　　"Wilt welcome."

Always Welcome

Do you sometimes struggle with depression, feelings of having "bombed out again," or of being no good? Charlotte Elliott, who lay in bed for 52 years, wrote, "God and he alone knows what it is, day after day, hour after hour, to fight against bodily feelings of almost overpowering weakness, languor and exhaustion, to resolve not to yield to slothfulness, or depression, but to rise every morning determined to take for my motto, 'If a man will come after me, let him deny himself, take up his cross daily and follow me' " (Kenneth Osbeck, *101 Hymn Stories,* Kregel Publications, 1982).

In her hymn Charlotte hints at what gave her the power to resolve day after day, to not let her feelings of depression control her but instead be able to rise above them. She wrote, "Just as I am thou wilt receive, wilt welcome, pardon, cleanse, relieve." Charlotte knew a welcome always awaited her.

I think of all the times I returned to Mother's home, first as a single young adult and later with my family. Mother always was watching for us and always came outside to greet us. I was always assured of being received and being welcomed. It never occurred to me that I couldn't return home; I knew I could.

Charlotte knew she could always "come home" to her Father. What if she had failed that day? She could let the past rest with her Father. He would forgive. Tomorrow she could try again. This brought a sense of deep security to Charlotte. From that security, in turn, she was able to pluck the flowers of courage and endurance, and to cast aside the weeds of depression, not because she knew that she should do this to be accepted by her Father, but simply because she recognized the weeds for what they were—harmful and destructive. As she learned, in Luther's words, to "accustom her troubled conscience to trust in God and not to tremble at the rustling of every falling leaf," she found power to assume command over enervating feelings of depression and order them to leave. Her experience can be ours too.

Loving, faithful Father, I come to you. Thank you that you always are ready to receive, welcome, pardon, cleanse, and relieve me. Teach me to use the power you offer to live triumphantly.

Day 5   Rom. 12:1-3   "Has broken ev'ry barrier."

Limitless Resources

Furlough time had come again for missionary Marian Halvorson in Tanzania, Africa. She could look back over the preceding years with joy. She had enrolled students in over 300 classes in the adult literacy program of the area where she worked. She had trained capable leaders to carry on. When she returned for her fourth term she would be free to move into a new work. But did she want to return? "I'm tired," she said to a friend, "tired mentally, physically, emotionally—and spiritually!"

"All of us feel that way sometimes," her friend said, "but perhaps you've been trying to do *yourself* what the Holy Spirit wants to do through you." Her friend laid her hands on Marian and prayed. Peace enveloped Marian. During the months that followed Marian learned to acknowledge her prejudices, accept God's forgiveness, and invite the Holy Spirit to exercise any of his gifts that God saw were needed for the common good.

Twenty-five years later Marian, who has gifted 20 African nations with her literacy training programs, and who continues to return to Africa to help with writing workshops for Christian educational materials, writes, "When God's Spirit is given the right to rule and use his gifts through us, amazing things do happen. But better than any miracle is the continuous anointing with fresh oil for every new challenge, task, trial, or difficulty. New ventures multiply. So do God's limitless resources."

Why then do we put barriers between God and ourselves, preventing him from giving us all the good things he has in store for us? Is it not because his love remains "unknown" to us? Of course, we know it in part—but only in part. We go our way, fearful to turn ourselves over completely to God and to let him call us, equip us, and give us whatever he wills. Because Paul recognized this inherent hesitancy on our part, he pleaded that in view of God's mercy we offer our bodies as living sacrifices, holy and set apart for God. Such a sacrifice, Paul stated, will be an act of worship and will please God.

Gracious God, break down my barriers of distrust. Teach me to trust the Holy Spirit to energize me.

Day 6   Rom. 6:13   "Now to be thine, yea, thine alone."

The Whole Half of Me

Many called the little African village a graveyard. It sheltered only those whose lives had been shattered by that dreaded disease, leprosy. Yet in that village where for so many hope and joy scarcely flickered lived Johan. Johan was always present for communion services. He would crawl forward and eagerly stretch out his fingerless hands to receive the bread and then with evident joy drink the wine. One day Johan shared with his pastor, Reuben Pedersen, the reason for his joy. The first glimmer of hope came, he said, when after his family had cast him aside, a nurse touched and washed his ulcers and cared for him lovingly. As he learned more about God from her, faith was born in his heart. Then he concluded, "Physically, there's only about half of me left, but I want to be sure that all of the other half of me serves God in every way possible."

Probably none of us are afflicted with leprosy. Perhaps most of us have whole bodies. But we all live with impairments or limitations of one kind or another—physical, mental, or emotional. We wish our health was better so we could do more. We wish we had had opportunity for a better education so more satisfying work could be possible for us. We wish our marriage was happier and our children less troublesome so we wouldn't have to spend so much energy coping with these situations.

The disciples lived with limitations too. Peter was not as educated as Paul, but that didn't stop him from witnessing and preaching. The place of leadership that women in the early church were allowed to take appears ambiguous, but we do know that a number of women like Aquila, Phoebe, Syntyche, and others just went ahead and did what they could.

Jesus bore the suffering our impairments or limitations cause us. But because he triumphed in his suffering, he can liberate us from paralyzing self-pity. Instead he can energize us as we yield ourselves to God, so we can use to the fullest what he has given us.

O Christ, help me accept my limitations and instead joyfully serve you with the "whole half" of me.

Week 5

Love Divine, All Loves Excelling

Charles Wesley, 1707–1788 Rowland H. Prichard, 1811–1887

1 Love divine, all loves excelling, Joy of heav'n, to earth come down! Fix in us thy humble dwelling, All thy faithful mercies crown. Jesus, thou art all compassion, Pure, unbounded love thou art; Visit us with thy salvation, Enter every trembling heart.

2 Breathe, oh, breathe thy loving Spirit Into every troubled breast; Let us all in thee inherit; Let us find thy promised rest. Take away the love of sinning; Alpha and Omega be; End of faith, as its beginning, Set our hearts at liberty.

3 Come, Almighty, to deliver; Let us all thy life receive; Suddenly return, and never, Nevermore thy temples leave. Thee we would be always blessing, Serve thee as thy hosts above, Pray, and praise thee without ceasing, Glory in thy perfect love.

4 Finish then thy new creation, Pure and spotless let us be; Let us see thy great salvation Perfectly restored in thee! Changed from glory into glory, Till in heav'n we take our place, Till we cast our crowns before thee, Lost in wonder, love, and praise.

37

thy	sal-va	-	tion,	En	-	ter	ev-	'ry trem-	bling heart.
its	be-gin	-	ning,	Set		our	hearts at	lib-	er-ty.
with-	out ceas	-	ing,	Glo	-	ry	in	thy per-	fect love.
crowns	be-fore		thee,	Lost		in	won-	der, love,	and praise!

Day 1   Rom. 8:1-17   "Love divine, all loves excelling."

Rules Don't Bring Peace

Susannah Wesley loved her 10 surviving children (nine had died in infancy), and applied herself with vigor to training them. Even Charles, the youngest, knew no slackening off of his mother's rules. Crying must be done silently, naughtiness astringently punished, kids to bed by eight, no snacking between meals, prayers morning and evening, six hours a day of home schooling from age five onwards, alphabet to be learned the first day of school, or else. Without question, rules and routine governed the Wesley home. In this atmosphere Charles grew up, toiling always to please God but never sure he was succeeding.

What a joyous discovery then to hear that God does not demand anything from us, but simply encourages us to receive the forgiveness of sins and eternal life he offers us. When this dawned on Charles, he could not contain his joy. "Love divine, all loves excelling," he cried out. "Fix in us thy humble dwelling."

The Lord heard Charles Wesley's cry. During a span of 50 years he wrote over 6000 hymns and sang the gospel into the hearts of people while his brother, John, preached. He died at age 81. A few nights before his death, he sang Isaac Watts's hymn, "I'll praise my Maker, while I've breath." He died with the words, "I'll praise . . . I'll praise," on his lips.

Lord, if we've been among those striving to please you by doing good, help us see the futility of this and instead hear your words of forgiveness and love pronounced to us.

Day 2   Matt. 4:16   "Joy of heav'n, to earth come down!"

No Christmas Tree

The sun, slipping behind the snow-covered Himalayas, was lengthening the shadows of the banana trees that encircled the courtyard where we sat. It found a space to peep through, and lit up softly the earnest brown face of the Nepali mother seated across from me. She flicked one of her heavy, black braids over her shoulder as she said: "We knew that Christmas is one of the great Christian festivals, but we didn't know the proper way to celebrate it. So we cleaned our house and put on a fresh mud floor. We swept the courtyard. The children brought cypress boughs and wild flowers from the forest. With these we filled our house, making it fragrant.

"We bathed and put on freshly laundered garments. Then Jetha, our oldest son, read from God's book the account of God's Son's visit to earth. We sang too, and the words spoke sweetness to our souls. And then we prayed. Thus we welcomed the Christ child, maybe not properly, but we did what our hearts told us to do.

"You see," she hesitated briefly, "we have not told you before, but we are believers in him. The first day I heard about him from you a great storm blew up in my heart. I knew I was hearing the truth, but I was afraid, so that I trembled, thinking of what this truth would cost me. At last I cried, 'Oh, God, I do not know you well enough yet to trust you without fear, but my heart tells me you are worthy to be trusted, and so you shall have me.' And that is why we celebrated this year the visit of God's Son to this earth. We maybe didn't do it properly, but we did what our hearts told us to do."

As I listened, I thought how it is possible to have every external sign of festivity and joyful celebration and yet not have a true Christian celebration, while those who have only recently come to Christ and know nothing about traditional customs can gather in true worship. And I thought how it is possible for the candles and the lights to blind our eyes, so that we can no longer see the true light, while those who have lived in darkness can see that light better than many of us who see mainly the glittering lights of this world.

O Lord, may the lights of this world not blind our eyes.

Day 3   Ps. 40:11-13, 17; Matt. 9:36   "Art all compassion."

We Need Arms around Us

In an Arizona hospice which shelters those slowly dying from cancer, a closely knit family had spent the morning reminiscing with their ill mother. From time to time laughter had filtered out to the hallway. Lunch time came. "We'll be back around 2:00," the family said. But shortly after they left, the mother began to gasp for breath. She rang for help and asked for Mary, her favorite nurse. "I'm dying, Mary," she said simply. Mary sat down beside her bed and held her hand. As breathing became more labored, the dying woman cried, "I think it would help if you would just hold me in your arms." The nurse folded back the bedclothes, and climbing into bed, gathered in her arms the bony body of the dying woman and held her until she gasped her last.

That nurse understood the meaning of compassion. Psalm 40:11 reassures us: "Thou, O Lord, wilt not withhold thy compassion from me" (NAS). The Hebrew word translated here, *compassion,* is feminine in gender. It means to treat with fondness, with gentle tenderness, to cherish, to care for as a mother cares for her helpless infant. In the Old Testament the word is used only in connection with God's tender care for his own, implying that his compassion far exceeds the compassion of any human being.

There is a Greek word in the New Testament that is also translated *compassion.* It is used repeatedly to describe Jesus' feeling when he looked at distressed people, whether he saw them as hungry, sick, or confused spiritually (see Matt. 9:36).

Is your situation such that you feel confused or distressed? Do you feel the need of God's gentle arms around you? Come to him and let him comfort you. His compassion never fails.

Do you know someone who needs to feel the security of God's arms enfolding him or her as you put your arms around that fearful one? Jesus was *moved* with compassion. Will we allow his compassion to move us too?

Thank you, O Savior, that you continue to be willing to bear our griefs and carry our sorrows. May we, in turn, be willing to bear the hurts of others.

Day 4   Mark 5:24-34   "Enter every trembling heart."

Healing Inner Hurts

Labeled unclean because of the menstrual problems that had drained vitality from her body the last 12 years, and knowing loneliness because her ailment kept her from entering a synagogue, this nameless woman was driven by desperation from doctor to doctor. Mark boldly states she "had suffered a great deal under the care of many doctors and had spent all she had, yet instead of getting better she grew worse" (Mark 5:26). But desperation keeps on hoping, and so, having heard about Jesus, she edged herself through the crowd until finally she could reach out and touch Jesus' garment. Instantly two things happened: she was healed, and she got caught!

"Who touched me?" Jesus cried, whirling around, scanning the crowd. The woman, realizing Jesus knew what she had done, came forward trembling and "told the whole truth," probably in bursts interrupted with tears expressing her loneliness, her anger, her worries about the future, her sense of helplessness. But when the woman told Jesus the whole truth, Jesus said "Go in peace and be freed from your suffering."

People sometimes carry around within them wounds caused because, in one way or another, they have suffered a great deal at the hands of others. But they have never dared tell anyone, and so the hidden wounds only fester and grow worse.

Why do we sometimes not tell the things that hurt us most? Why instead do our tongues release a motley host of small, inconsequential words? Why do we not let Jesus and others enter the locked rooms of our hearts? If we would only do this, we would hear Jesus saying to us, "Go in peace and be freed from your suffering." Our grief often would be lessened, sometimes gone, and always, always, the strength would be given to go on.

I need help to open the vacant rooms in my heart, O God.

Day 5   Ps. 16:6   "Let us all in thee inherit."

Claiming Your Inheritance

At long last the Israelites had taken possession of Canaan. Joshua carefully described their various inheritances. Some would receive forested mountain areas, others agricultural plains. Some were given lots that bordered the life-giving Jordan while the other lots ran along the coast, offering them opportunities for commerce and fishing. The Levites, however, would receive only towns to live in and pasturelands adequate for their flocks and herds, for the Lord was to be their inheritance. As Joshua told who would receive what, some grumbled. Others declared that "the boundary lines have fallen for me in pleasant places" (Ps. 16:6).

The hymn writer prayed that we all may claim the inheritance of rest God has for us. "What rest?" we ask. The rest we shall know after death, yes, but also the rest that comes when we stop striving and let Jesus live his life through us—the rest that comes with trustfully accepting whatever life brings.

Susan B. Krass, writing in *Lutheran Woman Today* (Sept. 1988), relates the lessons her severely retarded son Tom has taught her. After enumerating all the richness that Tom has brought, she goes on to say: "Because of Tom I've increased my ability to accept what is and what can't be changed. . . . There is a bittersweet quality to life with Tom. . . . There has been pain . . . yet I know that what I have experienced I might never have experienced and learned in any other way. Why such things have come to be a part of our lives is a mystery only God knows. But I do know this: Since this is the way things are for us, God uses our lives, our experiences, our circumstances as vehicles for God's grace. . . . I have also learned that for me 'good' is not wealth or fame or boundless optimism, but a growing realism about and appreciation of people and their circumstances. That good also includes the increasing ability to trust God with my own life and the lives of the people I love."

As we await the inheritance that will be fully ours after we cross the boundary line of death, what richer inheritance could be ours than the one Susan has described and appropriated?

O loving Father, help me to keep my trust fixed on you.

Day 6   1 Cor. 10:13   "Alpha and Omega be."

And All in Between

Carol's 23 years of struggling to live began when after her birth, grave-faced doctors told her parents she had been born with a congenital heart defect.

When she was two she underwent surgery that was only partially successful. At school playmates cruelly teased her because she was different. During her teen years Carol battled feelings of anger and self-pity. Malignancy of her thyroid meant a second surgery. Two years later open-heart surgery revealed she had no wall between the ventricles. "We can't help you," the doctors said sadly. Carol's troubles seemed to grow; she broke her knee and underwent further surgeries for appendicitis, an ovarian cyst, and finally, a tumor on her brain.

In between all this, she completed three years of college, earned her credentials as a dental assistant, and fell in love. Paul and Carol married. "Help me make Paul twice as happy in half the time," Carol prayed. They plunged into youth work. When a young girl ran away, Carol searched the hippy hovels along the beach until she found and brought home the girl. She introduced another girl who was on drugs to Christ and the girl was set free. Carol's last attempt to find medical help for herself came in 1971 when Carol and Paul flew to Houston for surgery on her heart. But 48 hours later Carol's struggle to live came to an end. Years earlier Carol had tucked in a corner of her mirror a slip of paper with these words: "Above all, we who bear his name must not be overcome by fear. He is our Alpha and our Omega."

Alpha is the "a" of the Greek alphabet and omega is the "z." Jesus is our Alpha and Omega. That is, he is the beginning and the end of life for us—and all that comes in between.

"I always pray with joy," Paul wrote to the Philippians, ". . . being confident of this, that he who began a good work in you will carry it on to completion until the day of Christ Jesus" (Phil. 1:4,6). If Carol could find Jesus sufficient for her beginning, end, and all that came in between, can we not also?

Sometimes it's the in betweens that are so difficult, Lord. Give me courage and strength.

Week 6

A Mighty Fortress Is Our God

Martin Luther, 1483–1546
tr. hymnal version, 1978

Martin Luther, 1483–1546

1. A might-y for-tress is our God, A sword and shield vic-to-rious; He breaks the cruel op-pres-sor's rod And wins sal-va-tion glo-rious. The old sa-tan-ic foe Has sworn to work us woe! With craft and dread-ful might
2. No strength of ours can match his might! We would be lost, re-ject-ed. But now a cham-pion comes to fight, Whom God him-self e-lect-ed. You ask who this may be? The Lord of hosts is he! Christ Je-sus, might-y Lord,
3. Though hordes of dev-ils fill the land All threat'ning to de-vour us, We trem-ble not, un-moved we stand; They can-not o-ver-pow'r us. Let this world's ty-rant rage; In bat-tle we'll en-gage! His might is doomed to fail;
4. God's Word for-ev-er shall a-bide, No thanks to foes, who fear it; For God him-self fights by our side With weap-ons of the Spir-it. Were they to take our house, Goods, hon-or, child, or spouse, Though life be wrenched a-way,

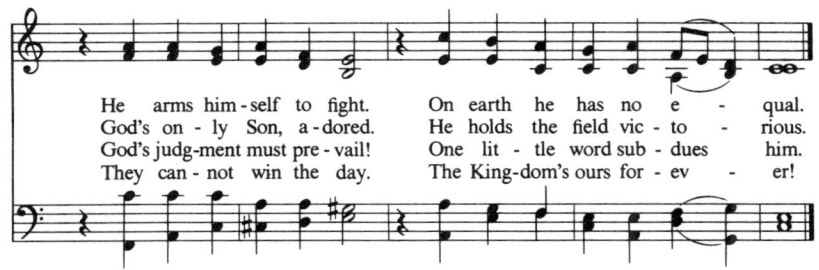

He arms him-self to fight.	On earth he has no e -	qual.
God's on - ly Son, a - dored.	He holds the field vic - to -	rious.
God's judg-ment must pre - vail!	One lit - tle word sub - dues	him.
They can - not win the day.	The King-dom's ours for - ev -	er!

Day 1   Psalm 46   "A mighty fortress is our God."

People Who Bring Security

Around the town of Wittenberg, where Martin Luther gained his fame as a preacher, ran a fortress. Did this prompt Luther, who liked to use figures of speech common to his listeners, to refer to God as our "mighty fortress" when he wrote this hymn?

Luther's first experience of God as a fortress probably came when his father sent him to Eisenach for his education. As many students did in those days, Luther went from door to door, singing and begging. His luminous, expressive eyes and melodious voice gained him entrance to the home and heart of a gentlewoman, Frau Cotta. Frau Cotta became a reflection to him of a loving, caring God. Not that his parents had not loved him; they had. But his miner father cherished lofty ambitions for his son, and his mother believed ardently in physical discipline. Once when the lad had taken a nut she beat him until she drew blood. Later, as an adult, Luther protested such harshness. "Where fear enters a man in childhood, it can hardly be rooted out again as long as he lives," he said.

Thus it was that Frau Cotta's home became for a time a fortress for Luther, a place of refuge from anxieties and fears, enabling him to enter joyously into life in a way he had not been able to do before.

As you think back over your life, can you think of homes and hearts that took you in, welcomed you, helped you see yourself as a person of worth and brought healing to wounds inflicted earlier in life? In turn are you willing to open the doors of your heart and home to troubled, anxious souls?

Give me a big heart that loves as you love, O God.

Day 2 Matt. 10:16-42 "With craft and cruel might."

When the Sword Pierces

After receiving his master's degree, to fulfill his father's wishes, Martin Luther began to study law. His father was taking immense pride in his son's accomplishments. However, under the seeming quiet of Luther's exterior demeanor, the waters were troubled. His mother's fear of devils haunted him. The severe punishment he had received as a child made him fearful of what would happen to him after death. Once, when washing his hands, he exclaimed, "The longer we wash, the uncleaner we are." Periods of depression began to torture him. He disliked the study of law. The death of a fellow student aroused more anxiety. At this point, caught outside as a violent thunderstorm struck, he flung himself to the ground and cried, "I will become a monk!" His father was furious. Four years later when, on the occasion of Martin's ordination, the monastery gave a banquet, his father came only grudgingly and sat grumbling. "I should much rather be anywhere else," he said. "Have you not heard a child should honor his father and mother?" When Martin protested he had received a call from heaven, his father retorted, "God grant it was not a lying and devilish specter." Those words stuck in Luther's mind and stirred up doubts as to whether he had made the right decision.

Years later Luther used to point out that one of the devil's tactics is to accuse and judge us. He speaks the worst of us and even takes what good we may do and twists it so it appears evil. Satan has used this tactic again and again when people want to follow Christ. "Do you not love your parents or your spouse?" he asks. "They do not believe as you do. Think how much pain you will bring them if you stubbornly choose to go this way." Perhaps never does the sword pierce quite as sharply as when our obedience to Christ causes pain to those we love. Jesus understood this. His response was simple. There is only one choice if we are to be worthy of him. Take up our cross and follow him and trust him to care for our loved ones.

Help those, O God, who have to make difficult decisions.

Day 3   Psalm 37   "A champion comes to fight."

In God He Trusted

Distressed because his ordination displeased his father, Luther's following months were heavy with despair. It didn't help that he spent them in a seven- by nine-foot cell with daily confession and introspection his main occupation. Fearing God's wrath, he began to practice every form of asceticism he knew. "God isn't angry at you," one of his superiors said. But Luther couldn't hear.

Staupitz, another superior, then arranged for Luther to teach biblical studies at Wittenberg. As he studied Romans and Galatians, Luther began to comprehend that he didn't have to earn merit with God; Christ had done it all.

The common people also recognized this to be good news when Luther began to preach it. They heard him gladly. At 31 he was appointed supervisor of 11 monasteries. His influence grew. Rome began to take notice when he denounced the practice of indulgences—selling forgiveness. Contributions to the well-padded church budget dropped drastically. Luther went on to denounce the teaching that peace of heart and personal salvation could come only through the pope and papal church. Alarmed, Rome took action, first trying to bribe him, then appealing to his loyalty to his vows, and finally, unable to force him to recant his statements, the church excommunicated him as a heretic. The emperor summoned him to a civil hearing. He went knowing he could be sentenced and burned at the stake. Instead, only his books were burned, and he himself banned from the empire. Later, at Augsburg an attempt was made to bring about reconciliation. Exiled at Coburg, Luther could not defend himself but relied on his colleague, Philip Melanchthon. He wanted it understood, he insisted, that he was not saying the Roman church was not a true church, but rather that it was not the only church, and that all who believed in Christ, wherever found and however governed, were members of the church universal. Rome would not accept this.

History has proven the validity of Luther's belief, and has left us a chronicle of how a man, during a troubled and dangerous time, found courage when he believed God was with him.

Give me courage, O God, to be true to my convictions.

Day 4   Eph. 6:10-18   "Devils fill the land."

The Deceiver

She crouched in a corner of her thatched hut, a pitiful, shrunken, aged Nepali woman, stark terror in her eyes. "They're at me all the time," she cried, referring to the attacks of demons who were harassing her.

The apostle Paul knew the reality of evil and evil powers. "Our struggle is . . . against the spiritual forces of evil in the heavenly realms," he wrote (Eph. 6:12).

Because Satan is a deceiver, he works in more sophisticated ways in the Western world: through lowered morals, pornography, permissiveness, addiction, discrimination, envy, jealousy, injustice, lust, greed, pride, doubts, mental and physical abuse. He also deceives through the lure of the cults, and by holding out alluring false promises to us—telling us we shall find satisfaction in success, wealth, pleasure, and popularity. The devil portrays sin as enjoyable and able to fulfill our desires, while actually sin poisons and—in the end—destroys. On the other hand—though it is hard for us to hear it—God says, "Sin will destroy, but if you repent, I will give you life."

Sometimes the evil one strikes ferociously. He struck before the founding of the Christian church when the infants were massacred after the Christ child was born. From that time on Christianity has been cradled in adversity. "The number of Christian martyrs throughout the 20th century is far higher than we have hitherto imagined," noted Dr. David B. Barrett. He predicts that a half million persons will lose their lives for Christ as a result of human hostility by the year 2000.

In the decisive battle of the ages between God and the evil one, we need to pray for perception to recognize his attacks. None of us will be exempted. All of us constantly need wisdom and spiritual resources to resist and overcome him. And to all of us comes the call to uphold in prayer those who suffer harsh physical abuse and devastating emotional wounds.

Look with pity, O heavenly Father, upon all who live with injustice, terror, disease, and death as their constant companions. Have mercy upon them. Help us to eliminate cruelty.

Day 5   1 Peter 5:8   "The old Satanic foe."

The Accuser

Peter compares Satan to a lion. The male lion snarls fiercely at the victim, distracting its attention while the lioness creeps up from behind, attacks, and kills. Satan too is crafty, distracting our attention so we are not even aware our spiritual life is being threatened.

Satan's object is to destroy life whether it is by inciting people to abuse, oppress, or murder others, or whether it is to destroy saving faith and produce despair.

How does he destroy saving faith and produce despair? He accuses and judges us. He delights to magnify our sin. "He converts a pardonable sin into an ocean and fire so vast that I do not know which way to turn," Luther said. "He can dress up death to look so terrible, horrible, and hideous that one completely forgets God and his Word," Luther noted. "Death he has often painted in such a manner that I could have died of fright" (*What Luther Says*, Ed. Edwald Plass, Concordia Publishing House, 1959).

Satan also seeks to destroy us by his very persistence. He "has sworn to work us woe!" Luther says in his hymn. He never takes a holiday. "If beaten, he rises again. If he cannot enter in by the front entrance, he steals in at the rear. If he cannot enter in the rear, he breaks through the roof or enters by tunneling under the threshold. He labors until he is in."

Even as Christ was not spared from the attacks of the evil one, so too we should not be surprised if Satan sticks around, accusing and terrifying us even as death approaches. A young man confided: "I had thought death for a Christian would always be serene and beautiful until I stood by the bedside of my dying father. Dad had been a faithful pastor for years, but so tempted was he to despair that again and again we had to reassure him of God's forgiveness, and because he was so weak, on his behalf we had to resist the devil. Finally the accusations ceased, and father died in peace."

O most loving Father, you want us to lay all our cares on you, knowing that you care for us. Protect us from faithless fears, and grant that no clouds in this mortal life may hide from us the light of your love shown in your Son, Jesus, our Lord.

Day 6   James 4:7   "We tremble not, unmoved we stand."

Sing the Devil Down!

The devil is like a fish, Luther once said. He views us as delectable bait, and so he circles until he can snap at us. But as he closes his jaws, he finds he has bitten into a hook and he is caught. That hook is Christ, Luther said, for he indwells us.

Though Luther knew he had to trust Christ to overcome the devil for him, still he recognized he had a part to play in fighting the battle also. He employed a number of tactics.

"One day," Luther said, "the devil came knocking at my door. 'Who do you want to see?' I asked. 'Martin Luther.' 'Well, Mr. Devil,' I said, 'I'm sorry to inform you that Martin Luther doesn't live here any more. He died quite a long time ago. Jesus Christ lives here now. Would you like to see him?' " And, Luther concluded, "that took care of the devil. He scampered off" (*What Luther Says*, Concordia, 1959).

Luther recommended talking back to the devil, but suggested that the conversation be kept brief. Simply say, "I am a Christian," he advised once. Or, "Begone, Satan! I want nothing to do with you." He also told his people to be well-armed with scripture and suggested they memorize passages like Galatians 1:4-5. "One little word subdues him!" he affirmed.

On numerous occasions Luther also used song to fight the devil. When the Diet of 1530 convened, anxiety gnawed away at Luther as he feared disastrous compromises. The death of his friend, Leonhard Kaiser, who three years earlier had been burned at the stake, still haunted him. "Nettles might be all right," he had tried to joke with a friend. "But fire? Ah, that would be too hot!" His father's and then his mother's deaths plunged him into grief. Questions tortured: was he right in the stance he had taken or was he leading people astray? Despair sat in the hallway, just outside his door. But remembering how he had told his people repeatedly to "sing the devil down," he would begin to sing this hymn—lustily!—until hope and courage returned.

When despair threatens to stifle us, we too may practice singing the devil down. It works; it really does.

Teach me, God, to turn to you in song during difficult days.

Week 7

My Faith Looks up to Thee

Ray Palmer, 1808–1887
Lowell Mason, 1792–1872

Day 1   1 Cor. 12:4-11   "My faith looks up to thee."

At the Price of Labor

Roy Palmer, the 22-year-old teacher, deeply stirred by a German poem of two stanzas, sat down to translate it into English. But after he had finished his translation, he found the words continuing to flow. Later he wrote, "I gave form to what I felt, by writing with little effort, four stanzas. I recollect I wrote them with very tender emotion and ended the last lines with tears." Palmer, a published poet, carried in his pocket the little notebook in which he had copied his poem. Then one day as Palmer was walking down the busy streets of Boston, he happened to meet Lowell Mason, the well-known composer from Georgia. "I'm compiling a hymn book," Mason said. "Do you have any poems I could set to music?" Palmer felt his notebook in his pocket. "Let's go in this restaurant," he said. "I have one here I'll copy for you." Thus "My faith looks up to thee" became a hymn.

Palmer had written his poem spontaneously and rapidly, but previously he had worked long, arduous hours perfecting his craft so he was ready when the moment of inspiration came. Although he was a descendant of John and Priscilla Alden, the poverty of his family forced him to leave home at 13 to work as a clerk in a store. During this time he became a Christian. Friends, noting his abilities and gifts, urged him to study. Eventually he graduated from Yale, taught, and then was ordained. But throughout all the years he had continued perfecting his skill as a poet.

Other hymn writers, poets, and composers have shared similar experiences of words or melodies flowing from them as though they were but channels. George Matheson did when he wrote, "O Love that will not let me go."

We may not write poetry or compose music, but whatever our gift, we need to remember the words of Leonardo da Vinci, "Thou, O God, dost sell us all good things at the price of labor." Whatever our gifts are, they are a trust from God. If we develop them faithfully, we'll always find a place where they can be used and be a blessing to others.

Give me perseverance to continue to develop the gift you have given me, O gracious Lord and giver of all good gifts.

Day 2   John 1:29-31   "Thou Lamb of Calvary."

Christ Died for All Races

John the Baptist, the son of a Jewish priest, grew up in a home where morning and evening his father sacrificed a lamb in the Temple for the sin of the people. John knew that the offering of sacrifices brought relief to sinners who longed to be forgiven. Out of this background John cried to the people as Jesus approached, "Look, the Lamb of God, who takes away the sin of the world."

What do these words mean to us? For many of us Christ's death on the cross has brought us the assurance of being forgiven and accepted by God. Perhaps, however, we have thought only of sins like lying, stealing, being unkind, etc. But Jesus, the Lamb of God, died to take away sin when it rears its head also in the form of racial supremacy, racial hatred, and persecution, and in the exploitation of other races.

How does Jesus take away sin when we think of it in this aspect? Has this not been a continuing process down through the ages? For in every age the unshirkable, unavoidable call has come to a few to boldly confront opposing evil forces. The call came to Martin Luther King Jr. "Injustice anywhere is a threat to justice everywhere," he declared. "Privileged groups seldom give up their privileges voluntarily." King saw his mission as one of "redemptive suffering, a bringing of the crucifixion into relation with the present society." For King, ultimately it meant a sniper's bullet.

Chances are we won't be called on to die. So then what is our role, our responsibility? Christ calls us to pray for all who work for justice, righteousness, and the end of discrimination. But he also calls us to action. "Christ calls us to personal repentance," Tournier wrote, "so that, forgiven and set free, we can throw ourselves into action." If Jesus died to take away the sin of all, how can we wait silent, not crying out for the deliverance of the jailed and jailer, the persecuted and the persecutor, the oppressed and the oppressor?

Strengthen, O God, all who work for justice for all people. Save the oppressed from hatred, bitterness, and despair.

Day 3   Isa. 40:31   "Strength to my fainting heart."

She Found Unknown Strength

When life plays rough with you, are you tempted to get discouraged? Do you grumble, wondering why you aren't treated better?

The psalmist David faced life realistically. Why, even a righteous man can expect to have many troubles, he said (Ps. 34:19). Illness, bad luck, accidents, heartaches, problems, death. These are the nitty-gritty ingredients of life. So why should we be surprised when they happen to us?

Perhaps we are caught unprepared because we have been shielded and protected too much in childhood. A dead pet or a broken toy is quickly replaced. Hospitals hide the sick from us. Extended care homes seclude the disabled old. The poor live in ghettos. We don't even rinse out messy diapers but throw them away. Our whole mode of life can contribute to softening us so we quickly forget this is part of what life is all about. However, David had an encouraging word too. *But,* he said, don't be anxious. The Lord will deliver you from all your troubles. How? By giving you the strength you need.

Florence Sande, a homemaker from Minnesota, discovered how true the words of this hymn were when her husband was crushed under a corn wagon, and she was left with three small children. Florence believed that somehow the Lord would see her through. The first test came when the pit outside into which the water from her automatic washer drained, caved in. It took two weeks to dig it out, but as she dug she repeated, "I can do it! With God's help I can do it!" She was forced to auction their farm machinery and livestock. The night before the auction the most valuable cow in the herd could not get up after calving. She knew they must get her on her feet or she would die of paralysis. The veterinarian, her father-in-law, and she tugged and pulled and finally succeeded. Wearily she tumbled into bed at 12:30 A.M. only to get up at 3:30 to milk the 35 cows. "But I found strength I never knew possible," she said, "strength for my fainting heart and physical strength."

This strength is available to us also in our times of need.

Teach me to trust you day by day and hour by hour, Lord.

Day 4   Genesis 45   "Life's dark maze."

God Prepares the Way

During the months immediately following her husband's death, Florence marveled again and again how God had prepared her. That first night when 35 cows faced her, ready to be milked, Florence gladly accepted offers of help from neighbors. "But we'll need directions for feeding them," they said. "Oh, God," Florence prayed silently, "forgive me when I used to rebel and feel resentful when I had to help in the barn because our hired men didn't show up. If I hadn't helped then, how would I know what to do now?" As she got out the records to check how much to feed each cow, she recalled a strange experience she'd had just a short while ago. Remembering the 35 cows by name always had been impossible for her. But one day she had looked at the cows with eyes that suddenly recognized each one individually. *How strange!* she had thought at the time. Now she understood.

In the weeks following she picked out of the mailbox bills, bank statements, forms from insurance companies, and other important papers, "Dear God," she prayed, "how thankful I am Arlen asked me to handle our business matters. Now I know how."

So it continued. Being able to see how God had prepared her brought reassurance to Florence that since God had shown her love in the past, he would never let her sink in her present troubles.

Florence knew how to look for and identify indications of God's love and care. Joseph did too. Though his brothers had sold him to strangers who brought him to Egypt, eventually he gained so much power that the Pharaoh made him prime minister. Under Joseph's astute planning, provisions were stored so when famine struck, Egypt could even sell grain to other nations. Thus when Joseph's brothers came, Joseph could sell to them and later give them a place to live. "Do not be angry with yourselves for selling me here," Joseph said, "because it was to save lives that *God sent me ahead of you*" (Gen. 45:5—italics added).

Loss is never easy to cope with, but it will be a little easier as we actively begin, every day, to think of and look for ways in which God has prepared us for what we have to bear now.

Open my eyes, Lord, to see in how many ways you care for me.

Day 5   Isa. 30:15   "Be thou my guide."

Finding Our Way Through

When middle-aged dairy farmer Olaf Olson went to bed one hot July night, he did not dream that within 24 hours both his arms would be dangling uselessly by his sides. Things had been going well. Oh, he had a little arthritis but what was that? So when pain in his neck awakened him he thought it was just arthritis. It wasn't. By afternoon the pain was gone, but so was the ability to use his arms. The doctor admitted him to the hospital and began tests. Then his sensory nerves flared back to life. For 30 days he writhed with pain. "I want to die!" he cried. "You must not!" Enid stubbornly said. "The children and I need you. Fight back."

Four months later a diagnosis was made: acute bilateral brachial plexitis, a rare nerve disease. No known medication. The disease would have to burn itself out. Would Olaf regain use of his arms? Maybe. Maybe not.

"We went back to our motel room," Enid recalls. "It was a dark, rainy day. The gloominess of the day matched the darkness within our souls. I took out my Bible and began to leaf through it. A tract fell out. I picked it up and read these words by F. B. Meyer: " 'Their strength is to sit still' (Isa. 30:7). Never act in panic. Calm thyself and be still, force thyself into the quiet of thy closet until the pulse beats normally and the scare has ceased to disturb. Wait upon God until He makes known His way. So long as that way is hidden, it is clear that there is no need of action, and that He accounts Himself responsible for all the results of keeping thee where thou art."

"Suddenly," Enid says, "I felt released and at peace. I knew that God would see us through."

He did. With physical therapy Olaf regained use of his right arm and learned to use the left in a supportive role. At 71 he is still farming. But wonderful as the physical healing was, both Olaf and Enid quickly acknowledge that the closer relationship with the Lord that resulted was worth far more.

In all crisis situations of my life teach me to look for you, O Lord, that I may learn to know you better.

Day 6   Isa. 43:1-2   "Fear and distrust remove."

Carrying On Despite Fear

Joy and contentment filled the first seven years of Kiyoshi Watanabe's marriage as Shigaru, his wife, bore him three children. But sorrow crushed the young parents when in two days' time disease attacked and killed all three little daughters. The birth of Miwa, a little girl, helped somewhat to fill the void. But later when Shigaru died giving birth to a son, Watanabe thought he could bear no more. Marriage to gentle, diminutive Mitsuko helped.

Then war broke out. Watanabe was stationed at an internment camp for Britishers in Hong Kong. When he saw the brutally mistreated prisoners, Watanabe cried out, "To despise, to mistreat, to hate like this, is not the way of God!" "So you are a Christian!" spat his superior. From that day Watanabe was watched.

Watanabe knew this. Still, he began to sneak prisoners' letters to relatives out of camp. He smuggled in medicines, vitamins, medical instruments, money, and serum for inoculations. Getting caught would mean death. Sometimes when he thought of this, Watanabe vomited or fainted. He kept hoping he would conquer his fear but he never did. Still he carried on. When he couldn't find words for prayer, he simply cried.

Then came the great blast at Hiroshima. Internment for Watanabe followed. In camp he longed for news of his family. One day the looked for, yet dreaded, letter came. Miwa, his daughter, had come the day before the bombing to take her mother away from Hiroshima. They were to leave early the next morning, but it wasn't early enough. For two days and nights Watanabe lay with his face to the wall. At last, little by little, he was able to accept what had happened, and forgive those who had dropped the bomb. He couldn't understand, but he was ready to trust God. If God had helped him before when he had been afraid, wouldn't God help now?

Few of us are called to bear as much suffering as Watanabe, or to perform acts of extraordinary courage. But though our testings are perhaps of lesser degree, still we all need courage. Hearing and reading the stories of those whom God has brought through the furnace can help us.

For brave ones like our brother Watanabe, we thank you, Lord.

Week 8

There's a Wideness in God's Mercy

Frederick W. Faber, 1814–1863
Early American

1. There's a wide-ness in God's mer-cy, Like the wide-ness of the sea;
2. There is wel-come for the sin-ner, And a prom-ised grace made good;
3. For the love of God is broad-er Than the mea-sures of our mind;
4. 'Tis not all we owe to Je-sus; It is some-thing more than all:

There's a kind-ness in his jus-tice Which is more than lib-er-ty.
There is mer-cy with the Sav-ior; There is heal-ing in his blood.
And the heart of the e-ter-nal Is most won-der-ful-ly kind.
Great-er good be-cause of e-vil, Larg-er mer-cy through the fall.

There is no place where earth's sor-rows Are more felt than up in heav'n.
There is grace e-nough for thou-sands Of new worlds as great as this;
There is plen-ti-ful re-demp-tion In the blood that has been shed;
If our love were but more sim-ple, We should take him at his word;

There is no place where earth's fail-ings Have such kind-ly judg-ment giv'n.
There is room for fresh cre-a-tions In that up-per home of bliss.
There is joy for all the mem-bers In the sor-rows of the head.
And our lives would be all sun-shine In the sweet-ness of our Lord.

Day 1   Psalm 103   "There's a wideness in God's mercy."

Campfire Testimonials

Once upon a time a strange thing happened. People were no longer bound to their own time periods, so all the people who have ever lived found themselves together at the same time. A goodly number of Yahweh's worshipers and Jesus' followers gathered for a weekend retreat in the mountains. The first night the stars were luminous and the moon sifted through the tall, sighing pines. The group clustered around a campfire to absorb some of its warmth. After they had sung some songs, the leader asked, "Who would like to tell how he or she has experienced the mercy of God?" One by one they arose to speak.

"My name is Ruth," the first woman said. "I met my husband when he was working in our country. When he died, I decided to emigrate to his country to care for his mother. I found myself a stranger in a foreign land. God had mercy on me. I met a good man who asked me to marry him, and we had children."

Another woman arose. "I too was a widow. My husband was one of the sons of the prophets. When he died, we had a lot of debts. I couldn't pay them. The creditors threatened to take my sons as slaves. God had mercy on me and met my needs so I could repay our creditors and keep our children."

Still another woman arose. "I had no husband, but many men sought my services, and that is how I earned my living. God had mercy on me and introduced me to his Son, Jesus Christ. His love for me dissolved my self-hate and taught me respect for myself. His promise of help released me from my feeling of helplessness. He changed my life completely."

A short man with squinting eyes arose. "I am the foremost of sinners," he said humbly, "but I received mercy that in me Jesus Christ might display his perfect patience."

And so the testimonies went on and on all through the night, for God's mercies never end; they are new every morning.

If you had been there at that campfire, what stories of God's mercies to you would you have told? Pause. Recall. Take time to do this. And then thank God.

For mercies past and mercies new we thank you, God.

Day 2   Matt. 5:43-48   "Earth's sorrows are felt . . . in heav'n."

Loving Ishmaels

Hagar, the surrogate mother, crouched by the spring in the wilderness. She was running away from the legal wife who had made life utterly wretched for her. Not that Hagar was without fault. She had ridiculed the childless Sarah. But now Hagar was afraid she and her unborn child would die. But God saw her, heard her, called her, gave her a promise, and told her to return to her mistress. She did.

Fourteen years later Hagar and Ishmael, her 13-year-old son, were again refugees in the wilderness. Hagar had known great astonishment when gray-haired, wrinkled Sarah had given birth to a child. Up until then Ishmael had been the recipient of all Abraham's fatherly love. When Ishmael saw Abraham bending over the baby, mimicking baby talk, he was embarrassed. Had not the two of them just forged a bond of manliness when they had suffered together through the painful rite of circumcision? And now all this fuss over a baby! Months later when Abraham threw a big party just because the baby was weaned, Ishmael exploded. He began to tease the little fellow.

Sarah was furious. "Get rid of that rascal and his mother," she ordered Abraham. Abraham was caught between the two women, but God's larger purpose had to be given priority. Hagar and her son had to go. Abraham grieved, but obeyed.

Abraham's and Hagar's sorrow was felt in heaven. God saw Hagar and Ishmael far out in the wilderness and saved them.

In the centuries that followed, Ishmael's descendants in large numbers turned their backs on Abraham's religion and became disciples of the prophet Mohammed. Still the God for whom past, present, and future are all the same, had not let that stop him from being moved by Hagar and Ishmael's sorrow. In our multi-cultural society, do you have opportunity to touch the lives of some Moslems and let God's unsurpassable love for them flow through you?

Teach me to love as you love, O loving God.

Day 3   Heb. 10:19-23   "Such kindly judgment giv'n."

God Is Easily Approachable

He stood, a red-haired, six-year-old, leaning against the door frame, rubbing his one leg with his other foot. He knew he had to tell his mother he had done wrong. He was scared, but he was counting on the kindness of his mother's justice. He had been through this before. First, there would be some kind of punishment or reprimanding—and he knew he deserved this—then his tears, his blubbering out, "I'm sorry," then his mother would open her arms to hug him and reassure him he was forgiven and that she loved him. At least that's what he was hoping for.

Fortunately, the little boy's mother lived up to his expectations. Fortunate indeed, for it often is from our parents we first learn that God, even in his justice, is kind.

Long before Frederick W. Faber wrote this hymn, the sweet singers of Israel were chanting the kindness of God. We may have missed how often they sang of his kindness, for the Hebrew word *tob* often is translated "good." But in its more distilled meaning, it means "kind." Kind in the sense of gentleness, a sympathetic kindliness, a sweetness of disposition that shrinks from causing another pain, a kindness that makes the person easily approachable.

"Give thanks to the Lord, for he is [kind]," the psalmist sang (Ps. 106:1).

The most renowned singer of all, King David, knew God was kind. Because he was so sure of this, he, like the little red-haired boy, dared to confess to his heavenly Father the awful, shameful things he had done. "Deal well with me for your name's sake; out of the [*kindness*] of your love deliver me," he prayed (Ps. 109:21). God did. God forgave David.

We too may be assured that we may always come to God just as we are. He will not reject us nor turn his back on us nor order us out of the home. Instead he will forgive and give us the chance to try again. Why then do we play pretend with him instead of being honest?

How great and beyond understanding is your kindness, O God!

Day 4   John 6:37   "There is welcome for the sinner."

Are All Welcome?

Someone asked an evangelist what he would have said if he had had opportunity to speak with Hitler. Without hesitation he replied, "I would have said, 'Mr. Hitler, Christ died for you.' "

That evangelist rightly understood the way Christ regards all, even those who destroy or harm those who believe in him. For Christ has no enemies. There is no one, absolutely *no one*, whom God does not love. In our Pharisaical attitudes *we* may shut out some, but Christ has only this to say to us: pray for them; love them. If I am ready to welcome them, can you do less?

But to say, "Christ loves you; Christ died for you," is one thing. Actually to welcome into our fellowship Hitlers who profess that they have become believers is quite another thing. Even the disciples had trouble with this. When the Lord in a vision told Ananias to go to Saul because he was praying, Ananias, in fear, protested. He had heard about Saul. But the Lord prevailed, and Ananias, trembling, finally went. But later when Saul sought fellowship with the Christians in Jerusalem, we read, "They were all afraid of him, not believing that he really was a disciple" (Acts 9:26). If it hadn't been for Barnabas who believed in Saul's change of heart and who pleaded with the other Christians to receive Saul, what might have happened? Deprived of love, understanding, and fellowship, would Saul have returned to his old ways? It's hard for us to picture this happening because Paul showed such single-minded zeal. But none of us can live in a vacuum devoid of love, and God's love most frequently becomes real to us through the love of others.

How is it with us? Can we welcome the one to our church who, for example, has served a sentence for rape but now professes faith in Christ? In situations like this Christ tests our capacity to love, welcome, and receive as he does. He also challenges us to believe in his power to really change lives.

I confess, Christ, that I find it difficult to respond with faith, love, and understanding in some of these situations. Forgive me. Help me.

Day 5   Rom. 2:4   "Most wonderfully kind."

Is This God's Kindness?

Everybody thought Ed and Nancy were the perfect couple. In spite of heavy demands at his office, Ed was exemplary in church attendance, served on the church council and youth committee, sang in the choir, and chaired the stewardship committee. Nancy also found opportunities in the church for her talents.

What nobody knew was that life at home was hell for them. The epidemic of "me-ism" sweeping the land had caught up with them. They competed with each other, were jealous of each other, resented and accused each other, demanded more from the other than the other could give, and engaged in shouting matches. And all the while they skillfully playacted in public. Finally, utterly miserable because of the hypocrisy of it all, Nancy walked out. Now the secret was known.

Then, liberated because they no longer had to pretend, Nancy and Ed sought help. Little by little each began to hear the voice of the Holy Spirit, reminding each of them where they had erred and how they needed to change. Eventually reconciliation came, followed by a stronger and more realistic relationship. What had seemed like such a cruel act on Nancy's part, God was able to turn into an act of kindness on his part, for "the kindness of God leads to repentance" (Rom. 2:4).

Why is God so eager to bring us to repentance? He knows the end of sin is misery, but misery is now modified because God continues to be kind and merciful to the good and the evil. But this misery will become sheer hell after death when those who have consistently chosen to put themselves before God and others will find themselves cut off from *all* God's mercies. So, because he is *kind,* God seeks to bring us to repentance.

Is there something in our lives that has been bothering us? Can we see this uneasiness as an act of God's kindness toward us? Why can we not bring to him whatever troubles us so he can help us make it right?

Forgive me, Lord, when I pretend to be better than I am. Help me to be honest with you, myself, and others.

Day 6   Rom. 5:6-11   "For the love of God is broader."

Needing and Giving Love

She was only seven, much too young to be sent away from home, but we had no choice. We were living in East Africa, and the nearest school offering an American curriculum was 300 miles away. She would be gone for three months, then home for a month. Every midterm we would travel the 300 miles to be with her.

On our first visit, as we were sitting outside watching the sports events, she climbed onto my lap. "I don't know why," she said, "but little kids just want to be with their parents."

I held her close. "And parents need to have their little kids around so they can love them too," I whispered.

Love is a passion with its origin in God, for God is love. Love is an intense emotion, compelling us to act. It may be felt as a need: Janet wanting to be close to me. Or it may be experienced as something given: I wanting to reassure her that we did indeed love her even though we had to send her away to school.

Love moved God to act, to give the most precious thing he had—his Son. Dare we say need prompted that gift, that, speaking in human terms, God was lonely and longed for someone to return his love? He could not help loving his people, for God is love. Yet as long as his children continued to turn their backs on him and refuse his offers of love, he could not experience love returned. How else could he show his children how much he loved them than by portraying it in real life? How else could he woo them back to himself? So he gave love, and as a result, his own need for fellowship and love was satisfied.

Both aspects are evident in our love life with God too. Sometimes we need him so desperately. We need to be reassured of his love for us. Other times we are so confident in his love that we just have to tell him how much we love him. Both types of love are authentic and acceptable. To both expressions God responds with joy. But always his love is "broader than the measures of our mind."

We stand amazed at your love for us, O God. Enable us to love you more purely and deeply.

Week 9

The Lord's My Shepherd

Psalter, Edinburgh, 1650   J. L. Macbeth Bain, c. 1840–1925, adapt.

1. The Lord's my shepherd; I'll not want. He makes me down to lie
In pastures green; he leadeth me The quiet waters by.
He leadeth me, he leadeth me The quiet waters by.

2. My soul he doth restore again, And me to walk doth make
Within the paths of righteousness, E'en for his own name's sake;
Within the paths of righteousness, E'en for his own name's sake.

3. Yea, though I walk in death's dark vale, Yet will I fear no ill;
For thou art with me, and thy rod And staff me comfort still;
For thou art with me, and thy rod And staff me comfort still.

4. My table thou hast furnished In presence of my foes;
My head thou dost with oil anoint, And my cup overflows.
My head thou dost with oil anoint, And my cup overflows.

5. Goodness and mercy all my life
Shall surely follow me,
And in God's house forevermore
My dwelling-place shall be.

Day 1   Psalm 23   "The Lord's my shepherd."

A Psalm for Today

In the first three verses of Psalm 23 we find the psalmist speaking to himself. Note also that the verbs he uses are in the present tense: "is," "makes," "leads," "restores," "guides," "fear," "are," "prepare," "anoint." In other words, this is a psalm for now, a psalm for today.

What were the four things the psalmist said he could worry about? The first was want. Not having enough for mortgage payments or the rent, for the children's education or medical bills. The second was death. Evil was the third cause for anxiety. Evil in its many forms: disease, earthquakes, storms, cyclones, crime, violence, hatred. And finally, enemies. Not only people who work against us and make life miserable for us, but all that causes us frustration and a feeling of helplessness.

As the psalmist enumerates all these causes for worry, he moves on to describe how worry thoughts can be dissolved as we experience the Lord as our Shepherd.

"The Lord is *my* shepherd," he says. When does a doctor become "our" doctor? When we go to him and trust him to care for our bodies. When does the Lord become "our" shepherd? When we go to him and trust him enough to let him care for us and free us from our worry about want, death, evil, and enemies.

"Wherever He may guide me,
　No want shall turn me back;
My Shepherd is beside me,
　And nothing shall I lack.
His wisdom ever waketh,
　His sight is never dim;
He knows the way He taketh,
　And I will walk with him."

—A. L. Waring

Day 2   Matt. 11:28-30   "He makes me down to lie."

Taking Time Off Is OK

A city of 2.5 million entrusted a friend of mine with the responsibility of setting up a business library. The commission included approving building plans, ordering furniture, equipment, books and periodicals, and hiring staff. The city also set a date when, with festive celebration, they would open the library. For two and a half years my friend worked long, wearying hours, and the library opened on schedule. "But," my friend wrote afterward, "seeing the library finally in operation did not give me a sense of achievement (whatever that means). I had such doubts about my work and my ability to provide effective leadership that I resigned. My superior, however, thought my feelings were caused by worry and stress and urged me to take a leave of absence and rest. That is what I am doing."

The Jerusalem Bible translates verses 2 and 3 of Psalm 23: "In meadows of green grass he lets me lie. To the waters of repose he leads me; there he revives my soul."

Some of us live with a sense of being driven in regard to our work. We feel our employers are imposing unreasonable demands on us. Voracious competitiveness in the business world harries us, threatening us, saying if we don't give all, we'll be left with nothing.

When God sees us living under this constant strain and stress, he grieves. He wants us to live in harmony with our bodies, minds, and spirits. *He* does not drive us. In contrast, he invites us to lie down when we need to do so. He says, "Take a little time off to play. You don't have to work night and day. Get to bed early enough so you can go to work the next morning with a song and not with a groan." Or, in today's language, we may paraphrase the verse and say, "Among the grass and trees of the park he lets me relax. He leads me to a weekend at a lake. There he revives my soul."

Free me, O Creator of the universe, from the compulsion to work, work, and work some more. Help me realize that lasting value lies in what I am becoming more than in what I am doing.

Day 3   Isa. 30:15   "The quiet waters by."

Our Noisy Interiors

Many of us today live far removed from gentle pastoral scenes of grass-carpeted, rolling hills and quiet waters, scenes that bring a sense of peace and tranquility to our troubled souls. Even if we are fortunate enough to live in an area abounding in lakes, so many homes and cabins encircle the lakes that human noises and the hum and roar of motor boats fill the air. Life is different for us than it was for David the psalmist.

We have to find our quiet waters within ourselves. But how difficult that is! We are so full of noise even when we are not talking. The noise is there when we worship, when our husband, wife, children, or friends want to talk with us. It's the noise of things we've done or said—sometimes in the far distant past that still bothers us. The noise of things we have to do today, tomorrow, or next week. It's so hard to get rid of all this noise and get quiet, really quiet inside. But until we do, how are we going to hear what our Lord has to say to us? Or what others want to say to us?

We may take comfort, however, that even great people of God have struggled with this problem. The story is told that St. Bernhard one day, in talking to a friend, complained that he couldn't even get through the Lord's Prayer without some distracting thought interfering. His friend was surprised. He was sure he could, he said. St. Bernhard proposed a bet that he couldn't. The wager was to be a fine stallion. His friend closed his eyes and began to pray, but before he had finished the first petition he opened them again and asked if the saddle also would go with the horse.

Martin Luther also admitted he couldn't get through the Lord's Prayer without other thoughts interfering. However, he said, "When thoughts come to me, I am glad if they go as readily as they came."

Thank you, gracious and understanding Lord, that even when we try to be disciplined, we live under grace.

Day 4   Matt. 14:6-14, 22   "My soul he doth restore again."

Burnout

With people and life constantly demanding so much from us, often we feel threatened with burnout. "Come unto me and rest." How we wish we could! But how? Telephone buzzing. People dropping in. Babies sick and crying. Junior falling down and ripping open his head. Endless committee meetings. Kids' school activities. We feel overwhelmed. Caught. Helpless.

There were days when Jesus and his disciples felt the same way. For example, remember when the disciples had just finished an exhausting schedule of meetings, only to return and hear the shocking news that John the Baptist had been killed—and in such a revolting way. "I think all of us need to get away," Jesus said. "Peter, can we take your boat?"

The trip across the lake was silent. But when they pulled up their boat to shore on the other side, Jesus sighed. Crowds again! They had followed him along the shore on foot. Could one never get away from them? There were sick to heal. Questions to answer. Even supper to fix for them. Finally, with the meal finished and the leftovers put away, Jesus called the disciples. "Take off, fellows," he said. "You need rest. I'll handle the crowds."

We read that he *made* the disciples get in the boat. Did Jesus not dare leave them with the demanding crowd because they had not yet learned to say no? Whatever the reason, after the disciples had rowed away, Jesus proceeded to dismiss the crowds. None of us would dare accuse Jesus of not being compassionate, and surely there must have been many unmet needs in that crowd, but Jesus knew his disciples' and his own needs. He remained in control of the situation. We may say he took the telephone off the hook, he disappeared for the day, he said no when asked to serve on yet another committee. And although Jesus "made" the disciples leave, more often he trusts us to have the common sense to understand when we've had enough. We *can* to a large extent remain in control of our situation. If we suffer from burnout, in most cases, we are at fault.

Teach me, O God, when to say no, when to get away, when to say "enough."

Day 5 Eph. 5:3-5 "Within the paths of righteousness."

Some Things Are "Off Limits"

The time was the first century. The Understudies of Diana, Inc., with headquarters in the Temple of Diana in Ephesus, in what is now Turkey, was making a special offer to the businessmen of the city. Easy loans. Free advice on business investments. Titillating thrills and tension relief for tired men. And as an added bonus, the men would be invited to a gourmet dinner, complete with the finest wines of the district. A hostess would serve them and entertain them with a musical concert, and afterward—if they wished—there were private rooms in back and the men would be assured that their wishes would be kept in confidence. The offers were made even more alluring by the pictures of long-legged, gorgeous women, clad in glamorous gowns, holding out champagne glasses. The fact that all of this would be carried out in a temple made it a sacred act, as well. No need to be concerned as to whether or not the transactions would please the gods. Diana could guarantee that she approved 100 percent.

So attractive and enticing had been the offers that even some of the Christians were exploring the opportunities offered. The apostle Paul fumed when he heard this. "Take a letter," he said to his secretary and dictated: "But among you there must not be even a hint of sexual immorality, or of any kind of impurity, or of greed, because these are improper for God's holy people. Nor should there be obscenity, foolish talk or coarse joking, which are out of place, but rather thanksgiving. For of this you can be sure: No immoral, impure or greedy person—such a person is an idolater—has any inheritance in the kingdom of Christ and of God" (Eph. 5:3-5).

The Good Shepherd leads his sheep only in paths of righteousness. If we're exploring other trails, we'll soon get lost.

Protect me, O God, from the dreadful error of self-deception. Preserve me from being squeezed into the mold of this world and the thinking and reasoning of this world. If I begin to drift away from you, call me back.

Day 6   John 14:2   "My dwelling-place."

No More Moving Vans

The year we returned from Africa for furlough Janet was four. During our year in the U.S. she became attached to her American home. But the day to return to Africa came. Midway through our flight to New York, she asked, "Can't planes ever turn around?"

We spent the night in Brooklyn with friends. The next day we boarded another plane. As it swept us into the white, billowy clouds Janet sighed, "Now I lose my home some more," she said.

I recalled that cry of anguish 20 years later when my mother died. With her death came the stabbing realization that her home would be sold. During all my wandering years, Mother's home had remained the one stable place for me. Now I too would "lose my home," my Minnesota, childhood home. I wept.

After Mother's funeral, seated on the plane for my return trip to my own home in California, I turned to Psalm 23 in my Nepali Bible. In Nepali the verb for *dwell* in the verse "and I will dwell in the house of the Lord forever" is in the continuous tense and carries the connotation of a dwelling that will continue on and on without end. I may be assured of a heavenly home with God that will never "get lost" for me. The pain and anguish of separation from loved ones, home, country, and our sometimes imagined or feared separation from God will be no more. For we read: "Then I heard a loud voice call from the throne, 'You see this city? Here God lives among men. He will make his home among them; they shall be his people, and he will be their God; his name is God-with-them. He will wipe away all tears from their eyes; there will be no more death, and no more mourning or sadness. The world of the past has gone'" (Rev. 21:3-4 JB).

Loving Father, with joy, I anticipate greeting you as you stand in the open door waiting for me.

Week 10

Rock of Ages, Cleft for Me

Augustus M. Toplady, 1740–1778
Thomas Hastings, 1784–1872

1 Rock of Ages, cleft for me, Let me hide myself in thee;
2 Not the labors of my hands Can fulfill thy law's demands;
3 Nothing in my hand I bring; Simply to thy cross I cling.
4 While I draw this fleeting breath, When mine eyelids close in death,

Let the water and the blood, From thy riven side which flowed,
Could my zeal no respite know, Could my tears forever flow,
Naked, come to thee for dress; Helpless, look to thee for grace;
When I soar to worlds unknown, See thee on thy judgment throne,

Be of sin the double cure: Cleanse me from its guilt and pow'r.
All for sin could not atone; Thou must save, and thou alone.
Foul, I to the fountain fly; Wash me, Savior, or I die.
Rock of Ages, cleft for me, Let me hide myself in thee.

Day 1   2 Cor. 4:7   "Let me hide myself in thee."

Imperfect Channels

Sixteen-year-old Augustus Montague Toplady did not know that when he wandered into a Dublin barn one evening he would come out a changed person. A layman was preaching. As the youth listened, the sins he had committed suddenly horrified him. But as he listened further and heard that Christ had died for him, his heart began to overflow with a warmth and glory he had not known before. That marked the beginning of a new life for Toplady, the author of "Rock of Ages."

However, Toplady's volatile temper remained a problem for him; it didn't disappear when he became a Christian. It continued to erupt. Some years later Toplady vented his anger against John Wesley, who was cautioning him against some extreme views he held. That angry explosion split the two men apart. For years Toplady nursed his grievances. Yet, in spite of that, he ministered effectively as curate, vicar, and minister of three churches. "How could this be?" we ask.

That is one of God's wonders. Even as we are saved by grace, so too by grace we serve, and by grace and grace alone, God blesses our efforts. In Paul's letters to the churches we read of no end of unlovely things that happened among the Christians: displays of selfish ambition, power struggles, envy, divisions, and immorality. Yet in spite of it all, the church grew.

So we too may take courage even though perhaps we often have wondered of what value we can be to God. We fail so often in reflecting his love and beauty. So much imperfection continues to reside in us. We so poorly interpret his love. But let us take heart. God will work through us, if we offer ourselves to him, not because of any merit or goodness on our part, but because his power is able to do great things through ordinary channels. He is eager to love and care for people by whatever means he can. Knowing this brings us joy and peace.

Thank you, gracious God, that you not only bear with, but work through, imperfect channels.

Day 2   Rom. 6:22-23   "Cleanse me from its guilt and power."

Friend Hair Shirts

To know Christ as our Savior is one thing. To live like a Christian every moment of every day is quite different. Sin lurks, ready to trip us whenever it can. Too often we stumble and fall. Too seldom do we know what it is to be saved from the power of sin over us. "How can we be freed?" we ask.

Dom Helder Camara, the beloved priest of the poor in Rio de Janeiro, related how he learned to let his spiritual nature take over (José de Broucker, *Dom Helder Camara*, Orbis Books, 1970). Drawing from the picture of the hair shirts that ancient saints used to wear next to their skins to mortify their selfish desires, he referred to the hair shirts that "God strews throughout our lives." "How hard it is for instance to encounter incomprehension and mistrust when one is sincere, and knows one's thought is being misinterpreted," he said. Then he added, "I often say that perhaps the best hair shirts are our friend hair shirts. In the life of everyone, sometimes in one's own household, there are persons who have the melancholy gift of shocking us a little by their mentality, their ideas, sometimes even by their tone of voice." Then Dom Helder said, "Ideally we do not let the person even imagine she is a hair shirt for us."

Some of us may object that that's not being honest. In reply Camara would say, "In each of us there is the old man and the new man. Why always be gentle and complaisant with the old one and not give the new man a chance?"

Paul made the same point when he talked about our being crucified with Christ. For Paul was not merely speaking about a theological truth we can appropriate for ourselves without it touching us. "Put to death therefore whatever belongs to your earthly nature," Paul commanded (Col. 3:5). Nail it to the cross. Painful? Of course. Hard on our pride? Incredibly so, but let's remember pride keeps us away from God. A terrible struggle? Most certainly. That's where our Gethsemanes come in. But to know deliverance from the power of sin, as Mother Theresa said, "We must have a real, living determination to reach holiness."

Help me to be willing to die to myself, O my Savior and Lord.

Day 3   Romans 7   "Not the labors of my hands."

Let the New Person Be in Charge

"It's all very well to talk about nailing my old selfish nature to the cross," we may object, "but I just don't seem able to do it."

The apostle Paul agonized over this too. "What I want to do I do not do, but what I hate I do. . . . What a wretched man I am! Who will rescue me?" (Rom. 7:15,24). And then he gives the answer, "Thanks be to God—through Jesus Christ our Lord!"

"But how, how, how does it work?" we ask.

It is true that our growth in holiness is dependent on our "real living determination to reach holiness." But, Mother Theresa also pointed out, growth comes through God's grace too.

We experience how that works when moment by moment, as different situations arise, we turn ourselves over to God and ask him to be in charge and live out his life within us. For example, a single young woman found it necessary, because of high rentals, to share an apartment with another young woman. "We soon discovered how different we were," she said. "I'm a morning person; she's a night owl. I'm orderly; she's 'casual.' I like quiet music; she, loud. I know I irritated her, and after a while she rubbed me so much, I couldn't stand it any longer. The turning point came when I learned every morning to say, 'New nature, given me by God, be in charge today! Look through my eyes. Listen through my ears. Be in control of my emotions.' And when I had had a good day seeing this work, I would thank the Lord and praise his new nature in me for having handled things so well."

"Put off your old self," Paul wrote (Eph. 4:22). "Put on the new self, created to be like God in true righteousness and holiness" (v. 24). While depending on God's grace, as we with discipline and practice let the new nature in us assume its rightful place and exercise control, that new nature will begin to breathe and live naturally through us. When that happens we will find ourselves much more relaxed and at ease, and really quite fresh, in one way, at the end of the day.

Give me the will, O God, to let go of my wish to have everything my way.

Day 4 2 Cor. 3:5   "Helpless, look to thee."

That "Nowhere-to-Turn" Feeling

How glad the Israelites had been to leave the Sin desert! But their hopes shriveled when they reached Rephidim. The burning heat had blistered and parched their lips and left them crazy for one thing only, water. Rephidim had none. The people growled and complained. "Give us water!" they demanded of Moses. Terrified, because he could see some of the Israelites already picking up stones, Moses cried out to God, "Help me!"

F. B. Meyer, in his book *Moses, Servant of God,* points out that heady success for Moses had preceded this crisis. "The parted ocean, the submerged enemy, the song of victory, the fall of manna, the evidence of his statesmanship and sagacity as a born leader of men—all combined to place him in an unparalleled position of authority and glory" (London: Marshall, Morgan and Scott, 1960). Few people can climb to positions of power or experience heady success without letting some self-centered pride enter their hearts. If Moses, because of his previous successes, had been tempted to believe he could handle the Israelites by himself, Rephidim taught him otherwise. At Rephidim Moses discovered how shallow was his people's loyalty toward God and him, and how ungrateful and uncaring they were—worse, how downright violent, dangerous, and treacherous they could become. Up against a situation over which he had no control, he cried out, "Help me!" God heard. "Take your staff and go to the rock at Horeb," he said. "I will stand there before you." It was as though God was saying, "I'll be there with you, Moses, to protect you. I'll meet your need." And he did.

Sometimes we find ourselves in terrifying situations, feeling everything closing in on us, smothering us. Difficult as it is to do, thank God for those Rephidims. We may think we can handle things by ourselves without God, but our Rephidims have a way of grinding down our pride. Without that happening, we may continue or wind up believing in our own virtue and ability apart from God and be lost forever. Instead, at our Rephidims we can experience afresh God's protecting power and his provision for whatever it is we need.

Help me remember, O God, that when I call "Help!" you'll come.

Day 5   Rom. 8:32   "Helpless, look to thee for grace."

Undeserved Love

"If God really cared, why did this happen to me?" Maybe all of us at some time in our lives have asked this.

The children of Israel, arriving at Rephidim, perspiration streaking their dust-covered faces, and thirst consuming them, angrily asked Moses that question. "Why did you bring us out of Egypt? Why did you bring us here to die?" They forgot who it really was who had brought them out. Not Moses, but God.

They also forgot that the journey, so far, really hadn't been unbearably difficult. They had traveled by easy stages to Rephidim. The cloud, representing God's presence, still hovered over them, the manna still fell every morning.

Was God tempted to be done with his doubting, complaining, demanding, insolent children? We read that afterward Moses named the place Massah, meaning "tempting God to slay us." Some referred to it as Meribah, meaning "argument" or "strife," a place where the Israelites had come in conflict with God. But if God indeed was tempted to destroy them—speaking in human terms—we may say he controlled his temper. We hear no words of anger spilled out. Instead once again God acted out of pure grace. He met their needs. Did they deserve it? No way! And he met their needs from an unexpected source. Even as a raven brought food to Elijah, and Magi from the East provided gifts which probably paid for the unplanned trip to Egypt, so too, for the children of Israel, when they needed it, water gushed from a rock.

And we, though undeserving, may trust God to supply our needs. At the same time we need to be prepared for surprises. God may supply them in ways we had never dreamed of. And as we thank him for his supply of these other needs, always, above all, we lift our hearts in thanksgiving for meeting our deepest need of all, the need for forgiveness and restoration with him, granted to us through the death and resurrection of Jesus. He who is called the rock offered his side to be cleft for us. The water and blood flowing from it have gifted us with eternal life.

Father God, you know our needs before we ask. Give us only that which you see to be best for us.

Day 6   Eccl. 8:7-8   "When my eyelids close in death."

If Our Feet Falter

I used to think I wouldn't be afraid to die. Numerous times I had lived through the death of loved ones and had had a couple brief, close calls myself. Writing on the subjects of grief and bereavement had led me to read many helpful books. I had pondered the subject. But I'll never forget the day in the doctor's office when, facing an undiagnosed physical problem, and noting my doctor's troubled face, I asked, "Is it serious?" My doctor, not one to unduly alarm his patients, replied, "I'm not saying you're going to die," he paused, and then continued, "but I'm not going to say you're not going to." Yipes! Suddenly I found myself profoundly scared. To my chagrin, I burst into tears. I regained control, but once at home I cried as I had never cried before. It was then I realized how completely I had fooled myself into thinking I could face death without fear.

Since then I have been comforted by the assurance that to fear to die is not un-Christian. Our will to live is usually very strong and rightly so. Death, in the New Testament, is described as the enemy, and even though Christ has overcome it, it remains the enemy. Even Christ, my Lord, was horrified by and drew back from the thought of death. "Father, save me from this hour!" he cried. Inherent in that anguished outburst undoubtedly was a shrinking back from having to suffer for the sins of the whole world (Who can comprehend that?). But that suffering meant death, physical death, and from this also Christ shrank. So then, need I be surprised if I experience fear?

True, not all experience fear. Just a few hours before the hymn writer, 36-year-old Toplady, died, he cried, "My heart beats stronger and stronger for glory. Death is no dissolution." But if when our time comes, and fear enters our hearts, we may pray for courage. And even if courage falters, with our trust anchored in Christ, we may be assured that we are secure, hidden in the rock cleft for us.

If my feet falter when I take the downward steps of death, give me, O Savior, your hand to hold, your strong Word to hear, and I'll attempt it well.

Week 11

Amazing Grace, How Sweet the Sound

Day 1   Psalm 51   " 'Twas grace that taught my heart to fear."

Grace Can Make Us Miserable

Turbulence and insecurity rocked John Newton's early life. The first upheaval came when his mother, who had taught him about God, died when he was only seven. His father, a shipmaster, then shipped him off to boarding school, but pulled him out when he was 11 to take him to sea with him. At 17 John enlisted in the navy. When he overstayed a shore leave, he was whipped and put ashore. He found passage on a ship, but it took him to Africa. A slave-trader offered him work. Newton accepted but found himself enslaved, half starved, and cruelly mistreated. Hungry, lonely, and confused, Newton turned to prostitutes for comfort. The emptiness in his soul only grew. Finally, at 22 he decided to flee and escaped on a boat going to London.

But God had not forgotten Newton. On board that ship Newton found Thomas á Kempis's book, *The Imitation of Christ*. The pure life of Christ awakened longings in him, but he despaired that he could ever live the kind of life God wanted him to. Still he wished he could. And when a violent storm raged for days but all were saved, he asked himself why God had saved them.

However, once safe in England he forgot all this and he, who had been the enslaved one, became the one to enslave. For six years he worked as captain of a ship that carried slaves from Africa to Britain. Still God did not give up, but caused Newton to become more and more miserable until at last he so despised himself for what he was doing that he abandoned his slave trade. Later under the preaching of Whitefield and the Wesleys, Newton's faith in Christ burst forth in full bloom.

We do not need to be slave traders to feel that we have really botched up things. All we need to do is ask ourselves: "What things about me, my thoughts and actions, and why I do them would I not want published in the papers or pictured on the TV evening news?"

But coming to an awareness of how we've sinned can be considered an act of grace if our need of forgiveness drives us to Christ. Grace made Newton miserable. But grace also relieved Newton's fears. Grace can do the same for us too.

When I despair because of my sin, help me turn to you, O God.

Day 2   Luke 15:3-7   "But now am found."

Who Searches?

God searches for us. What a comfort this is!

He searches for us even when we don't know we are lost. He found Adam and Eve in the garden, drawing up their own rules, and trying to make it on their own. He searched for Saul while Saul was still breathing out hatred against the Christians. Saul had absolutely no intention of becoming a Christian. Quite the contrary! But God found him. God searched for Hagar, a single mother, used by man and woman, and then cast aside like a dirty old rag and left to watch her child die. Hagar probably never dreamed God would care for someone no one else seemed to care about. But God did and does.

"I myself will search for my sheep and look after them." God says (Ezek. 34:11). "I will rescue them from all the places where they were scattered on a day of clouds and darkness. . . . I will search for the lost and bring back the strays. I will bind up the injured and strengthen the weak" (Ezek. 34:12b, 16).

Do we have loved ones who are not acknowledging God as their God? Some who don't feel a need for God? Others who are downright antagonistic or who make sneering remarks about Christians? Are there some who claim they don't believe there is a God? Maybe some are so burdened or engrossed with making a living that they have little time for church or prayer or reading God's Word, and we wonder how any flickering flame of faith that once was there can continue to burn.

Whatever the situation may be for those whom we love and long for, we may continue to trust God to bring them to himself. He is the Good Shepherd. He will seek them out until he finds them.

Thank you, faithful and compassionate Father, that you love our dear ones more than we do. In your own way and time seek them out and woo them back to you.

Day 3   Psalm 103   "How precious did that grace appear."

Shove in Some Shouts

Newton lived to see God bless his work abundantly. Yet even then he sometimes found it difficult to forget his early waywardness. His distress and sorrow over his former sinful life are reflected in many of his hymns and in the inscription Newton wrote which was placed at St. Mary Woolnoth Church in London.

> John Newton, Clerk,
> Once an infidel and Libertine,
> A servant of slavers in Africa,
> Was, by the rich mercy of our Lord
> And Savior Jesus Christ,
> Preserved, restored, pardoned,
> And appointed to preach the faith
> He had long labored to destroy,
> Near sixteen years at Olney in Bucks,
> And twenty-eight years in this church.

One of the strategies of the evil one is to get us to doubt God's Word. "Did God really say?" we find him sneering in the first recorded temptation (Gen. 3:1). The devil lies to us. He wants us to doubt that God has really forgiven us, that God cares.

But we need not listen to the whisperings of the evil one. Instead we should cling to God's Word. What does God say? "I, even I am he who blots out your transgressions, for my own sake, and remembers your sins no more" (Isa. 43:25). Can God lie? If God doesn't remember our sins, why should we?

"But I can't forget what I have done!" you may protest. Most of us can't. The thoughts may pop into our minds, but we need not dwell on them. We may not be able to forget, but we can choose not to remember. As Luther once said, we cannot stop the birds from flying over our heads, but we can keep them from building nests in our hair. So instead of focusing on our past sins, let us honor God by concentrating on his grace, his goodness, and his forgiveness. Or, as Billy Sunday once advised, maybe we should, "Yank out our groans and shove in some shouts."

Help me to believe implicitly in your forgiveness, O God.

Day 4   Romans 5   "Amazing grace."

The Many Faces of Grace

I sloshed through the rain along a rocky Himalayan trail. I was weary and weak, having just suffered through a bout of amebic dysentery (an internal landslide, as my mountain friends describe the malady). An emergency had summoned me to the town of Darjeeling 15 miles away. Rain ran down my forehead and into my eyes. My clothing was soaked and with each step my feet went squish inside my wet shoes.

The sight of a little wayside inn cheered me. I ducked under its overhanging thatched roof and collapsed on a crude, wooden bench. The innkeeper brought me a huge mug of hot, sweet tea. The men in the shop had stopped talking when I came in. One turned to me. Why was I out on such a dismal day? Where was I going? I told them. They clicked their tongues in sympathy. Then when I rose to go, one of the men came over and picked up my little suitcase.

"I will go with you and carry your case," he said quietly. "You are tired and ill, and I will help you."

"Is your home in the direction I'm going?" I asked.

He laughed. "No," he said, "in fact, it's in the opposite direction and down the hill."

I began to protest. He put up his hand. "If I want to help you, can I not do so?" he asked.

Thus my brother, though unschooled in the gospel, gave me an illustration of what grace means. For grace is God's gift given to one who does not deserve it and given freely with no expectation of return.

We are daily recipients of God's grace in many forms. God wishes us well, justifies us, forgives us, makes us his children, gives us new spiritual life, and gives us the peace that comes with a quiet conscience that is no longer anxious or feeling guilty. This grace is offered to each of us freely. All we need do is to do what I did with my Nepali brother's offer. I said: "Thank you. I am so grateful you will walk with me and carry my burden." And he did.

Thank you, Lord, that you will walk with me and carry my burden.

Day 5   Psalm 119:57   "He will my . . . portion be."

Positions Open: Sisters of Charity

Luverne and I had come to steamy, crowded Calcutta hoping to find Mother Teresa but she wasn't in town. Disappointed, we continued on our way. A few days later in another city a friend hearing of our wish said, "Mother Teresa isn't here either. Trying to track her down is as hard as catching a mosquito in the dark. But would you like to visit some of her nuns?"

Ah, yes, that would do. During the days following as we observed them at work in their hospice, talked with them, and roamed the streets looking for the dying, we learned about this now 77-year-old, bent, frail woman with the bad heart and her mission of grace. For indeed that is what it is. As of 1988 she had approximately 350 houses in 71 countries around the world. There her missionaries offer freely with no expectation of return the love they have for Christ as they care for the poor, the homeless, the AIDS victims, and the addicted. They feed, bathe, clothe, nurse, and most importantly, love them.

The sisters who remember Mother Teresa when she first came to India recall she was an ordinary person, extraordinary only in her deep prayer life. One of the outcomes of that prayer life was her hearing unmistakably, on a train going to the hill station of Darjeeling, God telling her to serve the poor by living among them. "It was an *order*," she says today. Because Mother Teresa years earlier had settled it that the Lord was to be her portion, there was no flinching, no hesitating before that command. Today the world knows the results.

Undoubtedly our service of grace will not be as dramatic, intense, or far-reaching as Mother Teresa's. But we too can be Sisters of Charity. How? Let's define the characteristics of a ministry of grace: well wishes for those who don't deserve it, offered in a concrete form that meets a need, but given freely with no expectation of return. Any ministry that has those characteristics can be termed a ministry of grace. The motivating force behind that ministry? Our love for our Lord whom we too have made our portion.

As I wait in prayer, make known to me your will, O Lord.

Day 6   Ps. 146:1-2   "As long as life endures."

Keep on Keeping On

Bereavement, sorrow, confusion, and hardship marked Newton's earliest years. Immoral living characterized his young adult years. But after his conversion experience, Newton began to experience God's goodness in so many ways: assurance of being forgiven by God, peace in his heart, the gift of a devoted wife who for 40 years constantly encouraged him, time to write over 300 hymns and the opportunity to publish them, and calls to parishes that rejoiced in his creative leadership. His ministry took on added meaning when a convert, Claudius Buchanan, became a missionary to the East Indies, and another convert, Thomas Scott, became a Bible commentator. Newton also developed a strong, supportive, and influential relationship with William Wilberforce and other political leaders who were linking forces to abolish slavery. His profound gratitude to God for saving him never ceased motivating him. "Retire," a friend begged him, shortly before his death. "Your health is failing and your eyesight. Slow down." "What?" old Newton almost shouted. "Shall the old Africa blasphemer stop while he still can speak? Maybe my memory is almost gone, but I remember two things: I am a great sinner and Christ is a great Savior!" (*101 Hymn Stories,* Kregel Publications, 1982).

Newton experienced God's goodness to the end of his life. His gratitude for God's grace kept him keeping on, faithful in whatever he could find to do.

The apostle Paul in prison in Rome, writing to the Philippians, admitted he really would rather "depart and be with Christ." Reading about what he had suffered (2 Cor. 11:23-29), helps us understand why he expressed this wish. But, Paul said, he believed he would continue to live a little longer in order that once more by visiting them he would be able to freshen and reinforce their faith. He would keep on keeping on.

How have you known God's goodness to you throughout your life? How are you experiencing it now? How are you offering him thanks for his goodness? Are you "keeping on"?

O generous God, teach me to not be weary but to continue on.

Week 12

O Love That Will Not Let Me Go

George Matheson, 1842–1906, alt. Albert L. Peace, 1844–1912

1. O Love that will not let me go, I rest my weary soul in thee; I give thee back the life I owe, That in thine o-cean depths its flow May rich-er, full-er be.
2. O Light that fol-lowest all my way, I yield my flick-'ring torch to thee; My heart re-stores its bor-rowed ray, That in thy sun-shine's blaze its day May bright-er, fair-er be.
3. O Joy that seek-est me through pain, I can-not close my heart to thee; I trace the rain-bow through the rain, And feel the prom-ise is not vain That morn shall tear-less be.
4. O Cross that lift-est up my head, I dare not ask to fly from thee; I lay in dust life's glo-ry dead, And from the ground there blos-soms red Life that shall end-less be.

Day 1   Luke 15:1-24   "O love that will not let me go."

God's Searching Love

Who of us can begin to comprehend that God, Creator of the universe, loves each of us individually, and because he does, he gently but persistently pursues us? He entreats us to become his beloved, to trust him, and to return his love. The story in Luke 15 of the father sadly letting his rebellious son leave home is preceded by two accounts of the shepherd searching for the lost sheep and the woman sweeping her floor looking for her lost coin—two stories that portray God searching for us. Most remarkably, God begins to woo us even when, humanly speaking, it would seem he sees little desirable in us.

Dorothy Day, declared by the historian David O'Brian to be "the most significant, interesting, and influential person in the history of American Catholicism," stormed through her adolescent and young adult years recklessly; she fell in love, became pregnant, had an abortion, and then began to embrace Communism. A common law marriage followed. Yet somehow Christ was able to reach her, and she found his love so irresistible and so surpassing any she previously had known that, forsaking her common law marriage, she made a love commitment to Christ.

Having done so, she began to discover that Christ was calling her—to borrow Leo Tolstoy's words—to throw out in all directions from herself an adhesive web of love, like a spider, and to catch in it all that came. Out of love for Christ she responded. Together with a fellow Catholic, Peter Maurin, she founded the Catholic Workers' Movement. In their network Houses of Hospitality they gave food, clothes, and housing to those in need.

We too may have experienced a time when, indifferent though we were to God, through some incident, word, or encounter, God called us to himself. After that, reaching out to others became as spontaneous and natural as breathing. Can we not then believe he is searching for those who now appear indifferent to him and that he will continue this search until he finds them?

Reach out through me, O loving Savior, and call to yourself those who do not yet know you but whose lives touch mine.

Day 2   Ps. 37:1-11   "I rest my weary soul in thee."

When Life Isn't Fair

Frances was sizzling mad. She had poured 35 years of loyal service into a corporation. With her employer, as his secretary, she had inched her way up until she occupied a spacious, private, thick-carpeted office on the second to the top floor overlooking a park. Then suddenly, when her employer retired, she was dropped down four floors to work in a noisy cubicle. Her salary dropped, too, and just when it would have counted most toward retirement benefits. A young woman with two year's experience was promoted to Frances's office and given a higher salary than Frances had ever received. "It isn't fair!" Frances stormed.

No, life isn't always fair. Sooner or later all of us make this painful discovery.

The psalmist offered helpful words for healing wounds when life treats us unjustly. First, he stated what not to do.

(1) Don't fret. You'll only waste energy. (2) Don't be envious. Chances are you'll need to pray for help to do this. (3) Resolve, with God's help, not to let your anger explode in public; you'll only hurt yourself.

Then the psalmist outlined what to do. (1) Commit your way to the Lord. Trust him. (2) Do good. If you can congratulate or help the young person upstairs, do so. (3) Delight yourself in the Lord. Remember your value to him is not dependent on your status or position. (4) Be still before God. Quit sizzling; listen to what he has to say to you. (5) Wait patiently. Maybe God has some surprises in the cubicles. Eventually Frances was assigned to a Christian manager whose family opened their home to Frances, who previously often had been lonely in her singleness.

"The meek," the psalmist insisted, "will inherit the land and enjoy great peace" (37:11).

Teach me, O God, to meet life's injustices in your way, that I may know peace and rest of heart.

Day 3   Psalm 91   "I yield my flickering torch to thee."

The Peace of Acceptance

Oh, that we could understand what peace lies in acceptance! How often we resent our lot in life! It takes spiritual maturity to realize that when we rebel we are questioning God's character, doubting his love for us, and denying his control.

But we can emerge triumphant from the testing by determining to remain true to what the Bible teaches us about God's character, even if what we see happening appears to contradict it. Kierkegaard referred to this. He said that from a rational point of view, when he thought of all the wars, imprisonments, and injustices suffered, and all the diseases and sorrows of this world, all he could say about God was that either he wasn't in control or he was cruel—intent on making people unhappy. But, he said, even as this was the only conclusion he could make *rationally,* still he would declare his intention to assert and believe that God is a God of love and does all out of love.

George Matheson, the author of this hymn, faced this testing when, at age 18, the poor vision he had suffered for years finally flickered out completely. What happened next we only know in part. Matheson wrote: "I was alone. It was the day of my sister's marriage, and the rest of the family were staying overnight in Glasglow. Something happened to me, which was known only to myself and which caused me the most severe suffering. The hymn was the fruit of that suffering."

But aided by his sister, Matheson went on to learn Greek, Latin, and Hebrew so he could pursue theological studies. He became pastor of a 2000 member church and wrote prolifically.

When, even in the face of all that seems to contradict it, we make a statement of faith to God that we believe he is in control and has only good planned for us, peace begins to overflow our hearts. That peace becomes the natural environment from which new life can come, life that will more than ever reflect brighter and fairer the one who calls himself the light.

If we find it impossible to make this statement of faith, let us not hesitate to tell Jesus so and ask his help.

I believe you love me, Jesus, and want only the best for me.

Day 4   1 Peter 4:12-13   "Seekest me through pain."

Offering Up Pain

Pain exists in all our lives. What we hope for is not always what we get. Tornadoes swoop and destroy. Accidents kill and injure. Businesses fail. Lovers divorce. Pain tears at and rips apart people.

Pain tells us that all, creation and all created ones in it, are suffering from brokenness, the brokenness that has come because of our broken relationship with our God. Because of this brokenness, as Paul Lindell expressed it in *The Mystery of Pain*, pain rightfully belongs in this world. "God has decided it shall be so. This is how he is handling the situation."

However, even though I accept the reality of pain, still I do all I can to alleviate it. But when nothing helps and pain persists, I will then try to do as editor Dorothy Faber said she sought to do during the 30 years she slowly died of lupus. "I admit freely that there were times that, in moments of intense pain or exhaustion from fighting pain, I have prayed for God to release me from the burden of my own body," she wrote. "But I didn't quit fighting, because I came to understand that our troubles are really a gracious sharing by God with us of His cross, that He is allowing us to take part in the redemption of the world in Christ by letting us carry small splinters of His cross. I came to realize that Jesus Christ, who was scourged and crucified for me, understands pain and suffering more than anyone who ever lived. With this realization came the understanding of the real meaning of the Incarnation. From that day forward, when my own pain came, I tried always to offer it to Him in thanksgiving for what He had done for me. If He could die for me, surely I could live for Him!" (*Presbyterian Journal,* September 1, 1982).

Others also have learned to offer their pain to God. Paul wrote in Col. 1:24, "I rejoice in what was suffered for you, and I fill up in my flesh what is still lacking in regard to Christ's afflictions, for the sake of his body, which is the church." Difficult lesson though it is, can we too learn to offer our pain to Christ?

Give me understanding of what it means to share your suffering, O Jesus. Help me view my pain as something I can offer you.

Day 5   Heb. 12:11   "I dare not ask to fly from thee."

Only Tightened Strings Bring Music

A missionary couple whom we affectionately called "Aunt" and "Uncle" stayed on and spent their early retirement years in East Africa. Carrying their violin and accordion with them, Aunt and Uncle kept busy visiting, teaching, and going to hospitals and the jail. Some of us were concerned about their jail involvement. We feared that former prisoners, after being released from prison, might look them up for undesirable reasons. Our fears proved valid. One day when our friends were not home, all their clothes were stolen from the clothesline, including Uncle's suit which was airing.

A few days later, while visiting us, they told us of the incident. I exploded. "You, of all people! You who give of yourselves so sacrificially. It isn't fair!"

Uncle patted me on my arm and said, "Why don't I play you a little tune?"

He bent down and opened his violin case, took out his violin wrapped in a soft beige cloth and unwrapped it. His face softened as he looked at it. Then he tucked it under his chin and began to tune the strings. One string stubbornly resisted producing a pitch that would satisfy Uncle. He sighed gently, took the violin from under his chin and addressed the string. "I'm just going to have to tighten you a little more," he said. "Then you'll sing sweetly. Understand?" He looked at me.

And in a flash, I understood.

Fr. Thomas Green in his book *When the Well Runs Dry* tells of the weddings of young people he has performed. "Each time I ask them to repeat the phrase 'for better or worse,' I wonder if they realize what they are promising," Fr. Green wrote. "I doubt that they do. We hope and believe it will all be 'better,' but if the 'worse' comes we think we shall try to survive it with God's grace. It never enters our minds that the 'worse' is not an obstacle to the growth of love, but it is just as necessary as the better" (Ave Maria, 1979).

I want to love you more, Lord Jesus. If this means learning to embrace loss and disappointments, then teach me.

Day 6 Rom. 5:1-5 "O cross that liftest up my head."

O Cross That Liftest Up My Head

What's it like to be a husband, and the father of a 13-year-old son and an 11-year-old daughter, and the pastor of a growing suburban church and know you are dying? For almost three years Pastor Robert Lange of Mission Viejo, California, knew.

Bob Lange died slowly, from his toes up. Paralysis crept upwards until it had him trapped in a cage so at last he could move only his neck and head and flip a finger or two. Bob knew that when this paralyzing monster, known as Lou Gehrig's disease, attacked one of his vital organs, he would die.

When life calls us to suffer, we experience in a new and more meaningful way the meaning of Christ's cross. It's as though we are being given the opportunity to enter into Christ's suffering, as though we can visualize our suffering pinned there on the cross with Christ. Because the cross is upright, we find our heads lifted up. What, then, does our suffering enable us to see?

Bob saw the necessity to make immediate, definite plans for the future of his family. Next, he saw the necessity of continuing to live as fully as he could. He used all the aids he could. He and his wife Magdalene resolved that, for the sake of the children, they would try to maintain as normal a routine as possible, and so she would continue to teach.

At church Bob revised his goals. He focused on encouraging initiative, creativity, and decision making on the part of his parishioners and handed over responsibility to dependable people. He sought to prepare them to cope with loss by sharing with them his temptations to doubt, fear, and be anxious, but at the same time he always pointed the way out. "Simply say, 'Lord, I need you. I need you as never before; help me,' and help will come," he said.

Throughout the months he would not tolerate self-pity either in himself or his family. Finally, when he could no longer work, he learned to accept help. Death came peacefully in sleep.

Sooner or later suffering will intrude our lives. When it does, we may remember the way Bob Lange allowed it to lift up his head, apply what we can, and be helped.

Give me wisdom and courage to live life triumphantly, Lord.

Week 13

When Peace, like a River

Horatio G. Spafford, 1828–1888
Philip P. Bliss, 1838–1876

1 When peace, like a river, attendeth my way;
  When sorrows, like sea billows, roll;
  Whatever my lot, thou hast taught me to say,
  It is well, it is well with my soul.

2 Though Satan should buffet, though trials should come,
  Let this blest assurance control,
  That Christ hath regarded my helpless estate
  And hath shed his own blood for my soul.

3 He lives— oh, the bliss of this glorious thought;
  My sin, not in part, but the whole,
  Is nailed to his cross, and I bear it no more.
  Praise the Lord, praise the Lord, O my soul!

4 And, Lord, haste the day when our faith shall be sight,
  The clouds be rolled back as a scroll,
  The trumpet shall sound, and the Lord shall descend;
  Even so it is well with my soul.

Day 1   2 Tim. 2:15   "Thou has taught . . ."

Growing Your Faith

Horatio G. Spafford couldn't believe it! His daughters dead? Only a couple of weeks earlier he had seen his wife and daughters off for Europe aboard the S.S. Ville du Havre. "Go to Europe for a vacation," their physician had ordered his wife, whose health was failing. Spafford felt he couldn't leave his job as professor at Lind University. "But go," he had urged his family. Now all four of his girls were dead. How could it have happened that another ship had rammed into theirs? He must get to his wife who had immediately been taken to Wales.

Shocked, dazed, and grieving, still Spafford was able to draw on his resources. For years he had taught church school. Preparing for his classes had led him to study of God's Word. Now portions of Scripture came to mind, strengthening him.

This was not the first time his faith had been tested. Years earlier the Chicago fire had reduced to ashes much of his property, but he had emerged stronger so that aboard the ship taking him to his grieving wife, Spafford was able to write, "Thou hast taught me to say, it is well with my soul."

While faith is a gift, still it is something we must develop. Nothing comes without effort. How can we build faith?

Spafford was able to draw courage from the Scriptures because he knew them. He had gained his knowledge largely from having to teach.

If you find it difficult to discipline yourself to study the Word, volunteer to teach a class. It's a wonderful way to learn.

Spafford had exercised faith earlier when fire had destroyed his possessions. He had learned that the more we use our faith the stronger it becomes (Heb. 11:8-12).

So snatch every opportunity you can to trust God. Thank him for difficult times. Feed your faith by study of his Word. Exercise it by obeying it. And watch it grow. Then when crisis comes, you'll be better prepared.

Create in me a hunger to know you better, loving Savior.

Day 2   Rom. 5:1-11   "It is well with my soul."

Not Merely a Feeling

Though plunged in grief because of the sudden death of his four daughters, yet Spafford wrote, "It is well with my soul." But the peace Spafford was referring to was not some transitory, unreliable emotion but rather the peaceful relationship that existed between God and himself.

How can we be assured that this relationship exists between God and ourselves? Let us turn to a word we can trust, God's Word. We read in 1 John 1:9, the first part, "If we confess our sins. . . ." Have we done this? Luther wrote, "Everyone is so constituted that he does not want the sin he commits to be considered sin" (*What Luther Says,* Concordia, 1959). To come to the place where we say, "I have sinned," is a work of grace.

But how can I possibly confess all my sins? some may ask. If God keeps a tape recording of all my thoughts, words, and deeds, and if he holds me accountable for them all, how am I going to be sure I've confessed all my sins?

This evidently troubled David too, for after he had confessed the specific sins about which the Holy Spirit had painfully reminded him, he gathered up all his other sins, known and unknown, and he made one big sweeping confession. "Surely I was sinful at birth. . . . Wash away *all* my iniquity and cleanse me from my sin," he cried (Ps. 51:5,2).

We may use Psalm 51 as our prayer of confession too. Our salvation isn't won by our confession after all, though at the same time, as Luther stated, God "does not want to forgive" those who do not acknowledge their sins.

However, Luther placed much stronger emphasis on God's forgiveness than he did on our confession. "I am completely steeped in, and saturated with, the article of the forgiveness of sins," he wrote. "Whatever a person may do, let him not think that as long as he lives here on earth, he will ever progress beyond the need of this forgiveness. In short, if God does not forgive sins without ceasing, we are lost."

Help me to be honest in confession and trusting in accepting your forgiveness, O God.

Day 3   Ruth 1:19-21; 4:13-17   "It *is* well."

He Could Have Rebelled

"If you'd gone through what I have, you'd be complaining too," Naomi said when she moved back to her home town after many years' absence. "First the rains failed, and the crops with them, and we lost our farm. Where were we to go? Elimelech thought we could make a go of it in Moab. Did he realize how far away 120 miles is? What it would be like to live in a foreign land? Then Elimelech up and died on me. I knew I had to find wives for Mahlon and Kilion. But how? All those idol worshipers around. Finally I found two decent enough girls. And then the boys died! As though I hadn't had enough troubles! No grandchildren, either, to care for me in my old age. Better head back home, I said. I sure hope somebody will care there. But don't call me Naomi. That means 'my delight.' Call me Mara. Bitter, bitter, bitter! That's how I feel about how God has treated me."

Like Naomi, Spafford could have rebelled and become bitter, but his hymn gives no indication that he did so. However, if we find ourselves rebelling when we experience loss, we may remember that rebellion is a common reaction. "Why did I have to have a stroke and lose some of my mobility?" "Why was I passed over for a promotion? It's like I say—get over 50 and no one wants you." "Why was I born with thick legs?" "Why can't I be beautiful?" The list is endless of the things against which we rebel.

But as long as we rebel, no peace will come. The path to peace is acceptance. Not resignation. Resignation is passive. Naomi was resigned. And bitter. Acceptance is positive, an active force. Paul Tournier, the Swiss doctor, pointed out in *Creative Suffering* that "accepting suffering, bereavement, and disease does not mean taking pleasure in them, steeling oneself against them or hoping that distractions or the passage of time will make us forget them. It means offering them to God, so that he can make them bring forth fruit" (Harper and Row).

But acceptance is so impossible that we cannot do it without God's grace, his enabling. Yet as with all acts of grace, God is more than willing to undertake for us if we only ask him.

Help me to accept that against which I have rebelled, O Lord.

Day 4   Col. 2:13-15   "My sin, not in part, but the whole."

All of It All the Time

The apostle Paul graphically describes how completely God forgives us. In Col. 2:14, Paul writes that the charges levied against us are wiped out. The picture he uses is of a credit record moneylenders used at that time. The record was entered on papyrus or vellum, a substance that was made from the skin of animals. Precious because not much was available, it was used over and over. When a debt was paid, the creditor simply would wipe off the ink. This was possible because the ink did not penetrate but simply sat on the surface. And so no record of indebtedness remained.

A contemporary example would be the slates with the plastic films on which we write. Lift the plastic film and the writing disappears. That's the picture Paul refers to when he says Christ has wiped out our sins. No trace remains. None at all.

This wiping out, this lifting of the plastic sheet to wipe out, is a continuous process. In 1 John 1:7 we read, "But if we walk in the light, as he is in the light . . . the blood of Jesus, his Son, purifies us from all sin." William Barclay translates the last part of this verse, "the blood of Jesus Christ is steadily cleansing us from all sin." Bishop Westcott noted, "The sin is done away; and the purifying action is exerted continuously." It's like standing in a shower 24 hours, constantly getting cleansed. Small wonder then that when Spafford grasped this truth he cried out, "Praise the Lord, praise the Lord! O my soul!" The joy and certainty of that forgiven, restored relationship with God, his loving Father, exceeded the deep sorrow he felt over the loss of his children. He was God's child. God would care for him. Any sinning of which he might be guilty during this stressful, awful time, God would forgive. God was constantly cleansing him. This brought a sense of deep peace which, in turn, would facilitate and allow healing to take place more rapidly than would be otherwise true. Have we, by faith, made this truth ours too?

How wonderful to be your forgiven child, O God! Thank you for the sacrifice of your Son that has made this possible.

Day 5   Phil. 4:7   "When peace . . . attendeth my way."

A Gift We All Can Give

I hadn't meant to say anything to my friend when I brought back a book I had borrowed, but suddenly all my fears of an upcoming surgery spilled out. Instantly she was on her knees beside me, holding me in her arms and praying. As she did, peace came that relaxed me so profoundly that later, to the astonishment of my surgeon, I experienced no pain following surgery.

Sometimes when the Bible speaks about peace it refers to the God-given feelings of calmness and relief from anxious fears that flow through us like a river.

"Peace! Do not be afraid," the Lord said to Gideon.

"Peace!" Jesus said to his disciples when he found them huddled together in fear of the Jews.

The opposite of peace is fear. When people are bereaved, in the first awful, tumultuous throes of grief they might fear they are going crazy. When husband and wife, bereaved of a child, begin to quarrel, they may fear their marriage is coming to an end. A widow may fear she won't be able to handle financial affairs or live alone. We could go on and on. Fears, in one form or another, raise their heads when we experience loss.

What can alleviate fear? A loving, caring presence, for one thing. During our traveling years as a missionary family, while we were on the road, I always used to sit by the bedside of our children until they were asleep. Just knowing I was there brought to them a degree of peace and security.

Jesus understood the importance of presence. When he was ready to leave earth, he assured his followers he would continue to be with them even though they no longer would see him. Note how many times in the Bible the words, "I am with you," or "I will be with you," are linked with "Fear not."

In many, perhaps most, cases, we experience God's presence with us in the presence of his children. Being with those who love us can bring calmness, peace, and courage. We can offer this too to troubled souls. All we need is to be lovingly available, believing God will give them his peace.

Make me an instrument of your peace, O peace-giving God.

Day 6   James 4:7   "Though Satan should buffet."

Handling That Old Serpent

The devil had to get in his two cents worth. *Buffet* is a strong word meaning to push around, to knock down, cuff, and ram.

Spafford knew how to handle Satan. Do we?

Of first importance is to believe that he really exists. Nothing would delight Satan more than to have his existence, and thus his presence, denied. Then he really can confuse. The Bible, from beginning to end, is straightforward in speaking about the Evil One's existence. Satan was so real to Martin Luther that once when Satan was harassing Luther, Luther finally picked up an ink bottle and threw it at him.

Next, we need to recognize what Satan wants to do: destroy us (1 Peter 5:8). He begins by eroding our trust in God. To Spafford he whispered, "Why continue to trust God? How can God love you and allow this to happen? Turn your back on him."

Now, although we never treat Satan lightly, at the same time we remember he already is defeated. Christ has overcome him.

"Why should you be afraid [of the devil]?" Luther asked. "Do you not know that the prince of this world has been judged? He can do no more than a bad dog on a chain, which may bark, run here and there, and tear at the chain. But because it is tied and you avoid it, it cannot bite you."

But how will we get him to leave when he comes?

Jesus used the Word of God to reply to him. Notice in Matthew 4 how three times Jesus said, "It is written." When the devil says, "God doesn't love you," we can turn to God's Word and use it against him. When he tempts us to break a commandment, we can remind him that God has said, "Thou shalt not," and that means *thou shalt not.*

And finally, let's shift our focus from Satan to God. Let's begin praising God and thanking him that he has set us free from the power of Satan. For some reason, the devil just can't seem to stand it when we praise God. Try it.

When temptation comes, help me to be wise and strong, Lord.

Week 14

In the Cross of Christ I Glory

John Bowring, 1792–1872
Ithamar Conkey, 1815–1867

1. In the cross of Christ I glory, Tow'ring o'er the wrecks of time. All the light of sacred story Gathers round its head sublime.
2. When the woes of life o'er-take me, Hopes deceive, and fears annoy, Never shall the cross forsake me; Lo, it glows with peace and joy.
3. When the sun of bliss is beaming Light and love upon my way, From the cross the radiance streaming Adds more luster to the day.
4. Bane and blessing, pain and pleasure, By the cross are sanctified; Peace is there that knows no measure, Joys that through all time abide.

Day 1   Phil. 3:3-16   "In the cross of Christ I glory."

We Glory Not in Gifts

Statesman, philanthropist, poet, writer, naturalist, business man, linguist—all are titles we could give to Sir John Bowring. By the end of his life he had studied 200 languages and could converse in 100. He used this skill to translate works from 22 languages. But he himself also wrote 36 volumes: economics, history, poetry, natural science, travel, biography, finance. His brilliant mind explored field after field. His versatile abilities opened doors for careers as a political economist in Holland, France, and Belgium, a member of Parliament, a British consul at Canton, a Minister Plenipotentiary to China, and finally a governor of Hong Kong. Queen Victoria knighted him when he was 67. After retirement from government posts, he vigorously pursued a life of writing and speaking. This, then, was the man who wrote, "In the cross of Christ I glory."

Bowring's life story calls to mind the apostle Paul's. To his friends at Philippi Paul wrote, "we . . . glory in Christ Jesus, and put no confidence in the flesh—though I myself have reasons for such confidence" (Phil. 3:3-4). Paul then enumerates what he could take just pride in: his family tree, his religious upbringing, his personal religious zeal, and high morals. In a letter to the Corinthians, Paul wrote about the hardships and sufferings he had endured for Christ, so severe and numerous few could equal them (2 Cor. 6:4-10; 11:6—12:13).

Paul did not discount the worth of what he had done. God had given him much. He had simply tried to be a faithful steward in using what had been given him. But Paul's glory was not in what he had done, but in Christ from whom he had received all, and who had given him the most precious treasure, eternal life.

Acknowledging the gifts God has given us is not pride. Using them to the full is simply being a responsible steward. And receiving honor graciously is also something we can do because we know, as Dag Hammarskjöld expressed it: "The gift is God's—to God." Our glory resides in Christ and his cross.

Teach me to receive with joy and to use faithfully the gifts you have given me, O God.

Day 2   Acts 4:33   "Tow'ring o'er the wrecks of time."

Why Is the Cross Remembered?

Some writers trace the inspiration for this hymn to a visit of Bowring to Macao, a harbor city on the South China coast. A bronze cross on the top of a massive wall caught his eye. He discovered it to be part of a cathedral the Portuguese had built years earlier. A typhoon had leveled the cathedral, leaving only this one wall with the cross atop it standing.

But more substantive reasons lay behind Bowring's conviction that Christ's cross towers "o'er the wrecks of time." His work had led him to many countries and prompted a study of history, religions, and cultures. Yet he steadfastly maintained that Christ and his cross towered above all, for, as he stated once, "Christ is all we know of God." When all else had fallen, Christ's cross had remained, offering a faith for the world.

What has made the message of Christ and his cross so indestructible? Read through the book of Acts and notice what the disciples talked about most. It was Christ's resurrection. That was what gave to Christ's cross a different value and status from all the other thousands of crosses that were erected during those barbarous and cruel days. For the cross had proven powerless to keep Christ dead. He had died, but after three days, he who was life had walked out of the grave, not just a spirit, but a being in a recognizable, touchable form. When they saw him, the disciples were beside themselves with joy. What he had said was true! Being alive, he had overcome it for himself, and so they could be assured he had and would overcome it for them too. Every Sunday they celebrated, and on the first anniversary of Jesus' resurrection, Easter, they celebrated as they had never celebrated before. Such joy and such spunkiness in the face of danger they had never known before, and so contagious was it that it spread and spread down through the centuries. And it is this glad news that Jesus lives that keeps his cross towering high, offering hope when all else crumbles.

Restore to me the joy of my salvation so that joy may set my feet running to witness of you, my risen Savior.

Day 3   Revelation 21   "Hopes deceive and fears annoy."

When Hopes Deceive

Five years is a long, long time to live not knowing if your husband is dead or alive. During the war in Vietnam Carole was one of the women who faced that ordeal daily. She did so with outstanding Christian faith. Since there was no word of his death, she was sure he was alive somewhere. Still sometimes her faith wavered. It happened once on a dull, rainy morning. But Todd, her five-year-old son, seeing her tears, determined to cheer her up. "Come see what I've made!" he begged. In his room he showed a house he had built with his blocks and lifted off the roof. Inside was a plastic soldier. "There's Daddy!" he cried. At that Carole really began to cry. Todd was dismayed. "Don't feel so bad, Mommy," he comforted, "God's there too."

Two more years passed and then the message came. Todd's father wouldn't return. It was verified he had been killed. Hope had deceived Todd and his mother.

How often hopes deceive! Naomi had hoped when her sons married, a secure future would be hers. Her sons died. Jesus hoped Peter would be a rock. To begin with he was as unstable as sand.

We too know the chill when personal, cherished hopes disintegrate. And on a larger scale we hope and long for a more just, peaceful, and safe world. To legislate and work for justice, and to alleviate distress is our Christian duty. But we must always remember we wait for the eternal kingdom God alone will set up. Otherwise hope will deceive us again. As Karl Barth reminds us: "We have a unique, revolutionary hope to proclaim to this world, but we have no system of economic or political principles to offer which would presume to present in itself the content of this hope. There are only Christian decisions as signs of hope. For God himself and him alone, is this hope."

Sometimes those living in countries where freedom is restricted understand better than we do that their hope rests in God alone. Together with Carole, Naomi, and Peter, they probably treasure it more than we do too.

Teach us, O God, to place our hope in that which will not deceive.

Day 4   Phil. 4:6-7, 19   "Never shall the cross forsake me."

Resources for Every Need

Years ago a dear friend and I enjoyed an unusually satisfying relationship. We turned to each other when in need and trusted each other. We were able to confess to each other some of the despicable garbage we discovered hidden within us, knowing the one would not condemn the other. And so it was I always came away from my times with my friend feeling cherished, wanted, and that I had worth.

Then cancer attacked my friend's brain. Before her battle came to an end, my friend's personality changed. She became hostile, accused me of laughing at her, of not caring for her. Her stream of complaints and accusations grew longer and more insistent. And I found myself coming away from our visits, not enriched, but ground to dirt, and when I dared to admit it, I didn't even like her anymore. Then it was I who had to turn once again to the Lord to appropriate his forgiveness and his grace and power to persevere in loving when my love no longer was returned.

Older people who become more and more helpless and isolated sometimes become hostile even towards those they once loved. Women (for women far outnumber men) in full-care units especially need help. Because they are unable to get out and because they lose their last vestige of privacy when they are forced to share a room with a stranger, they sometimes suffer bitterly. But for us to be able to continue to visit and love them when love is not returned may call for more than we have to offer, humanly speaking. It is precisely at times like this that Christ's cross does not forsake us. As we are willing to be hurt, we shall find that his cross actually lifts and carries us. And though the nails may pierce us too, still through that cross comes life. We pray that it will come to the one to whom we are ministering, but if, at least to our eyes, we cannot see it breaking through the walls they have erected, it can come to us.

Thank you, Jesus, that when our flame of love for another flickers and threatens to go out, you will fan it for us again.

Day 5   Isa. 45:9   "Pain . . . by the cross [is] sanctified."

The Hammer and Chisel

Pain and tragedy rudely interrupted Bowring's highly successful life in China when the bread put on his family's table was laced with arsenic. His wife died from the poison.

The age-old question arose. Why did this happen to one who sought to do only good?

Friedrich von Hugel, writing in *Selected Letters,* noted: "Christ came and he really did not explain it [suffering]. He did far more. He met it, transformed it, and He taught us how to do all this, or rather He himself does it within us, if we do not hinder his all-healing hands" (Dutton, 1927).

An acquaintance of mine who is a sculptor spends years on every work. First the idea is born, then the musing as to how to develop the idea. Sketches. Then a small scale model, followed by a larger scale so more and more details can be worked in and faults observed. Only after painstaking preliminary work is the final work begun.

Thus the master sculptor works with us. He knows the finished design he wants to come up with; he dreams of producing a likeness of his own beloved Son. The work begins. The small testings start the chipping away process. As the testings proceed, and we do not resist, more and more the figure he has hoped to chisel out emerges.

God reaches out and takes every form of evil that touches us and uses it as a means of molding and shaping us. Often it's painful. Who wants to be hammered or chiseled away at? Yet, if we could only see the Master's hand on the hammer and chisel and realize what he is after, we'd realize he is paying us a great compliment by choosing to work on us. He is taking meticulous care with us; and if we cry out to be left alone, it means we are asking for less care, not more, less love, not more.

Help me not to get off the sculptor's block when the hammering and chiseling takes place, O God.

Day 6   Psalm 100   *"Joys that through all time abide."*

Let's Celebrate!

A National Geographic television special portrayed the rugged life of Scandinavian fishermen. Gone sometimes for six months, their return home always calls for a family feast. Three generations may gather. The finest clothes are worn, the whitest cloth put on the table, the best-loved food served, and a most elegant dessert is brought in as the crowning finale. The remainder of the day is spent in visiting, playing table games, looking at family albums, listening to the men's tales of their last perilous voyage, and then eating some more.

Sorrow shared is sorrow lessened. Joy shared is joy enhanced.

Feasts in the Old Testament were appointed times set aside for sacred joy. Under the Mosaic law the people observed three annual festivals. Jesus introduced the sacred feast of his Supper. The first Christians observed each Sunday as a celebration of Easter, and as time passed, they added more and more commemorative dates to the calendar, all of them occasions of sacred joy. Jesus' cross and resurrection had occasioned all this celebration for the early church and still does for us today.

Festivals and celebrations create golden memories, one of the few things most of us can retain even when life strips us of most everything else. As church families, as extended and nuclear family units, and as clusters of friends, we do well to look for occasions to celebrate. And having Christ as our unseen guest at our feasts enhances our joy, for where his presence is felt, people find it hard to continue cherishing grudges or refusing to forgive. Knowing him also makes us more capable of entering more freely and fully into even everyday joys, for his life within us sharpens our sensibilities. Christ and his love for us, revealed on the cross, makes our blessings more blessed and our pleasures more pleasurable.

You have been so good to us, O God. Teach us to celebrate your goodness to us more often and more joyously.

Week 15

I Know that My Redeemer Lives!

Samuel Medley, 1738–1799, alt. John Hatton, d. 1793

1. I know that my Redeemer lives! What comfort this sweet sentence gives! He lives, he lives, who once was dead; He lives, my ev-er-liv-ing head!
2. He lives triumphant from the grave; He lives eternally to reign; He lives exalted, throned above; He lives to rule his Church in love.
3. He lives to grant me rich supply; He lives to guide me with his eye; He lives to comfort me when faint; He lives to hear my soul's complaint.
4. He lives to silence all my fears; He lives to wipe away my tears; He lives to calm my troubled heart; He lives all blessings to impart.

5. He lives to bless me with his love;
He lives to plead for me above;
He lives my hungry soul to feed;
He lives to help in time of need.

6. He lives, my kind, wise, heav'nly friend;
He lives and loves me to the end;
He lives, and while he lives, I'll sing;
He lives, my Prophet, Priest, and King!

7. He lives and grants me daily breath;
He lives, and I shall conquer death;
He lives my mansion to prepare;
He lives to bring me safely there.

8. He lives, all glory to his name!
He lives, my Savior, still the same;
What joy this blest assurance gives:
I know that my Redeemer lives!

Day 1 1 Corinthians 15 "I know that my Redeemer lives."

Graves Will Be Tenantless

When Paul talked to those who didn't believe in the resurrection, he didn't just say, "The Bible teaches it; believe it!" Instead, he argued.

Christ's resurrection was a historical fact, he said. God's justice demanded it; good must be rewarded, evil punished. Christ's claim that he came to save people included not only their souls but their bodies, which otherwise would perish with death. Our bodies, he stated, would be refashioned and become like Christ's resurrected body (Phil. 3:20-21; 1 Cor. 15:49).

And finally, Paul stated, our hope in the resurrection is embedded in God's promise. Can God lie and still be God? No, Paul declared.

When our faith wavers, we can also remind ourselves of those whom Christ raised from the dead: the daughter of Jairus (Matt. 9:25), Lazarus (John 11:43-44), and the widow's son (Luke 7:14-15). Will it be any more impossible for Christ to raise us than it had been for him to raise these others? we may ask ourselves.

But in the end it is a declaration of faith we make when we say we believe that the day will most certainly come when all the graves will be tenantless. And before that stupendous event, at the time of our death each of us shall go to be with our Lord. Just what that means I am not sure, but I rest my faith on Jesus' words spoken to his disciples the night of his crucifixion. "I will come back and take you *to be with me* that you also may be where I am" (John 14:3). That is enough for me.

Thank you, God, that through the death of your Son you have saved us from the hopelessness of death.

Day 2　　Eph. 1:1-14　　"He lives to silence all my fears."

Welcome Home

"You have been here merely on a brief visit," a Chinese Christian father said to his teenage daughter who lay dying. "If the time has come for you to go home, go home in peace."

"I go, Father," the daughter whispered, "and may our Lord be with you and give you peace."

What enables a father and daughter to say this? I think Helmut Thieleke has given us the answer. "The real point of death is no longer parting from, but homegoing to," he said. "I will remain in the fellowship of him who is the Alpha and Omega, the Beginning and the End. With this knowledge I go into the night of death, which is a real night, because I know who is waiting for me in the morning."

What does it matter then, as we stand at the grave of a loved one, or face our own death, if we feel the storm blowing around us? What if day has become night and all nature around us seems to be in mourning? What if our eyes try to see lights in our Father's window but can only trace the faintest outline of the house itself since our eyes are so blurred with tears?

And yet, and yet, do we not fear the passage? Most of us do. But when fear creeps in, we can make George MacDonald's prayer our own:

"To Thee a new prayer I have got—that when Death comes in earnest to my door, Thou woulds't Thyself go, when latch doth clink, and lead him to my room, up to my cot. Then hold Thy child's hand, hold and leave him not, till Death has done with him forevermore.

"Till Death has done with him? Ah, leave me then? And Death has done with me, oh, nevermore! He comes and goes to leave me in Thy arms, nearer Thy heart, oh, nearer than before! To lay Thy child, naked, new-born again of mother-earth, crept free through many harms, upon Thy bosom, still to the very core" (*Diary of an Old Soul*, Augsburg, 1965).

Day 3   Rev. 21:1-7   "He lives to wipe away my tears."

God Bears Our Sorrows

Terry and Barbara Morgan had waited to have their first child until Terry had completed his education. How overjoyed they were then when Barbara became pregnant! Months passed. The end of her pregnancy approached. Unexpectedly, Barbara started vomiting. "Better get a sonogram and X-rays," her doctor said. "Get back to your doctor," the sober nurse in the X-ray department said. While they waited to see their doctor, Terry said, they were "cloaked in dreadful unknowing," which became a shocking, horrifying knowing when their doctor gently told them Barbara was carrying a child with a gross congenital defect. Part of the skull and forepart of the brain would be missing.

"We learned that such children were born alive but doomed to die after only a few hours. We felt as if we were trapped in a bad dream," Terry related.

That afternoon marked but the beginning of grief and sorrow for Terry and Barbara. They felt flawed, like outcasts. When the baby was born, they couldn't bear to look at her. Only later did they name her.

"Slowly," Terry said, "I began to grasp that God is no *sender* of sorrows, but *sharer* of sorrows. Because of our faith in Christ we believed we could look forward to that day when all the cracks in creation will be healed, cracks that now allow things to enter and break babies and bring disease and disabilities and death."

Some years later Terry faced another tragedy. As Barbara approached her 40th birthday, dark clouds of depression, which she carefully hid from Terry, closed in upon her. A note she left assured him she knew he loved her, and she, him, but she could not go on living.

Barbara's tragic death painfully jolts us to the realization that only in eternity will all the cracks in our hearts caused by bereavement be fully healed. Till then we who survive must try to look to Jesus to bear with us our sorrows and carry our griefs and enable us to go on living as long as we live.

Teach us, suffering Savior, to let you bear our sorrows.

Day 4   1 Thess. 4:13-18   "He lives, and I shall conquer death."

A New and More Elegant Edition

When was the last time you planted seeds to raise flowers or vegetables? You may have trouble remembering. Most of us, instead of planting seeds, tuck nursery seedlings into the soil. Only three or four percent of our nation work as farmers, and experience the awe and wonder of seeing, in response to seeds buried in the soil, whole fields waving in golden celebration or standing at attention in tall rustling green rows. Sad really. Our grandparents who farmed had a much more realistic attitude toward death. I don't think many questioned the reality of life after death either. But as we have lost touch with the near-magical ability of soil and water to transform seeds into an entirely different form, doubts about the resurrection of our bodies have crept into our minds too.

How can it be, we ask? Everyone knows our bodies eventually become a few bones and a fine dirt-like substance. The Chinese in Hong Kong are powerfully aware of this. There, because of lack of land space and in order to make room for the newly deceased, family members exhume the bodies of deceased loved ones after seven years and put the remains in a jar. How can those ashes, that clay, become a body again, we wonder.

Faced with death, our own or that of a loved one, we need God's enabling grace and his revelation to enable us to believe that one day the corruption of our bodies will give way to incorruption. We need to know weakness will give way to power and our bodies, previously activated by lung-breath and heart-beat, will be quickened to new life by God's Spirit. God will bring this faith to birth in our hearts if we ask him. He did for Benjamin Franklin, who composed this epitaph for his tombstone:

The Body of B. Franklin Printer
(Like the cover on an Old Book Its contents torn out
And stript of Lettering and Gilding) Lies here, Food for Worms,
But the work shall not be lost,
For it will, (as he believ'd) appear once more
In a new and more elegant Edition
Revised and Corrected By the Author.
When my faith falters, help me, O God, to trust your Word.

Day 5　　John 14:1-6　　　　"He lives my mansion to prepare."

Sharp Eyes and Quick Ears

Join me in a brief exercise of the imagination. Our aged mother has died. As we arrive at the mortuary for the visitation, a visibly upset mortician greets us. "I'm so sorry!" he stammers. "I can't understand it. Someone has stolen the body!"

"Stolen the body!" we cry. Incredulous, we approach the casket. It *is* empty. Only a gold wedding band lies on the white cushion. "Dreadful!" says the mortician. "I've called the police."

Stunned, we return home. We plug in the coffeemaker and sit down around the kitchen table. And then suddenly Mother is there, filling our cups. We gasp. She laughs.

"See," she says, putting down the coffee pot and pirouetting, her face rosy with health and joy exuding from her entire being. "The paralysis is gone. And the pain. Tell my friends. And you, my dear ones, don't weep for me. I'm whole again!" And with those words she is gone.

Why have I asked you to join me in this fantasy? Simply because we've heard so often the story of Christ's resurrection and it has become so commonplace that we need to put our imaginations to work and catch the joyous wonder of it. While the Bible isn't too specific on details, we can gather some facts. We know we shall not suffer from disease, pain, poverty, hunger, thirst, cold, or heat (Rev. 7:16). "The body will have sharp eyes," Luther wrote, "so as to be able to see through a mountain, and quick ears so as to be able to hear from one end of the earth to the other."

Will we know each other? Moses and Elijah, on the Mount of Transfiguration, were identifiable. Jesus' resurrection body was recognizable and still bore the marks of crucifixion.

Relationships to each other will change. Sin will have no power over us. The transformation of our characters will be completed (2 Cor. 3:18). But most important, we shall come to know God as he really is (Matt. 5:8; 1 John 3:2). Our relationship to him will be one of love and intimacy (1 Cor. 13:12).

Strengthen our faith in the hope of our resurrection, O God.

Day 6   John 5:19-29   "What joy this blest assurance gives."

What If Only Once?

Too often we stumble and falter, wondering if the resurrection of our loved ones or of ourselves actually will take place. We realize if this were to happen it would be the most stupendous of all miracles. Can God actually perform this seemingly unbelievable miracle? we wonder.

Let's think of it this way.

What if only *once* in our lifetime we saw the miracle of a seed planted in the ground bursting forth into a prickly bush that produced an exquisite rose? What if in our age only *one* woman gave birth to a child? Can you imagine the headlines in the newspapers? Or only *once* was the sky set aflame with a lingering sunset or only *once* did a moon suddenly hang luminous and silent in the black night sky? Or only *once* did rain fall? Only for *one* day did the sun shine. Only *once* did birds, who up to that time had been flying around silently, suddenly burst into song.

If all these daily miracles, which have become so commonplace that we take them for granted, happened only *once,* would we not stand open-mouthed, astonished, overwhelmed. Yet we are continually surrounded on every hand by miracles.

Why then should we doubt that the day will come when only *once* in history, even as Christ's birth, death, and resurrection were once-in-history happenings, so too at one time in history the great miracle of resurrection will take place, and we, you and I, will participate in it? What a day that will be!

God of all grace, you sent your Son, our Savior Jesus Christ to bear our sin. We thank you that by his death Christ destroyed the power of death. We thank you for your promise that as Christ rose from the dead, we too, after death, shall one day live as he lives. Make us certain in our hope of the resurrection. To you be all honor and glory, now and forevermore.

Day 1   Ps. 40:2-3   "O my soul, praise him."

He Had to Write Songs

Joachim Neander couldn't help it. Jesus Christ had just become real to him. The joy that filled his soul had to overflow in songs of praise. No matter if his Reformed Church for 150 years had confined itself to singing psalms set to metrical tunes. No matter if the heads of his church believed that people could not properly worship God using words written by men and women but must use only words from Scripture. He, Joachim Neander, had to express his joy, and so he began to write hymns of praise. His own church turned its head to begin with, but the singing Lutherans enthusiastically welcomed his hymns. Slowly the Reformed Church recognized what it was missing, and their people began to sing Neander's hymns as well as those of others.

What had preceded Neander's outburst of song? Though he was fifth in a line of distinguished clergymen in his family, young Neander had decided he would have none of what he considered a stuffy life. Instead, when he was 16 he began to really "live it up." Then when he was 20 something happened. He had talked two fellow students into going with him to a service at St. Martin's Church. The three had intended to gather fresh material to laugh and scoff at later. But Neander had not reckoned with the power of the Holy Spirit. When the pastor, Theodore Under-Eyck, preached that day the result was that, as one commentator expressed it, "he who came to scoff, remained to pray."

In the decade that followed Neander wrote 60 hymns, most of them hymns of praise. And as he dared give expression to the joy he knew, he freed the people of his church to use the words of others and their own words to express their love.

Living daily in a right relationship with God should occasion outbursts of praise from us too. If praise of our God is sparse in our lives, maybe we need to ask ourselves what's gone wrong. For praise, like prayer, should be as natural and vital to our spiritual life as air and breathing are to our physical lives.

Tune my heart to sing your praise, O God.

Day 2   1 Cor. 1:10-17; 3:1-9   "Now to his temple draw near."

Belonging

When is bread true bread? Is it white or brown or speckled? Does it come in loaves, rolls, or flat? Is it plain all the way through, or is it plain on the outside and filled with goodies inside? Is it quite tasteless except for the vegetables and meat enclosed in it? Does it go by the name of Limpa, Pita, Sourdough, Bagel, Danish, or Lefse? When is bread true bread?

Many new converts ask the same question about the church. Which is the true church? Spurning the Limpa or Sourdough on which they had been raised, they go searching for a better bread.

Joachim Neander searched for a brief time. He was serving as rector of the Latin School at Dusseldorf, working under an abrasive supervisor. A separatist group attracted his attention. Neander stopped attending services in his own church and started meetings in his home. He and his followers began to judge who were Christians so they could admit only those they deemed Christians to the Lord's Supper. The Church Council at Dusseldorf finally decided they would have to dismiss Neander. After 14 days Neander asked to be reinstated.

Even as it sometimes takes us years to grasp the value of our biological family, so sometimes it may take us years to appreciate the value of our church family. Some don't take the time to look for it but join another family. Perhaps in some instances this may be the wisest move. The most important thing is to be sure we become part of some visible, local church family. We need what a group can offer us. We need to listen to differing perceptions and insights. Our church family also can offer us love and understanding, can pray for us and lend support in times of crisis. Our church family may fail us in some respects, but so does our birth family. But overall our church family will do a pretty good job caring for its family members and especially if each member does his or her part. If we are to live a life worthy of our God, we need to have a "temple" to which we, along with others, can draw near to corporately praise God.

Thank you, God, for the wonderful gift of a church family.

Day 3   Matt. 17:1-21   "As on wings of an eagle."

Nudged Out of the Nest

Our five-year-old son refused breakfast. He shook his head at lunch too. "What's wrong? Are you sick?" I asked. "Naw, I'm fine," he said and slipped outside to play. But by midafternoon hunger won out. As he sat on a stool in our kitchen devouring a peanut butter sandwich, he paused midway to ask, "Know why I didn't eat today?" "No. Why?" He gulped down some milk. "Well, yesterday when I climbed up on your lap, you said, 'Goodness! you're getting so big, pretty soon I won't be able to hold you on my lap.'" He eyed me and then finished in a rush of words, "And I don't ever want to get that big!"

We smile. And yet are we not often like my son? We don't ever want to get so big we have to venture out and confront the big, bad world. Politics are too messy. Working with those addicted to drugs and alcohol too disappointing. Providing listening ears for the distressed too emotionally draining. Confronting injustice too risky. "Here's my check," we say. Or, "That's not my cup of tea." Or, "I know someone who can do the job better than I."

When we persist in refusing to be the salt Jesus wants us to be, God sometimes acts like a mother eagle. He gently pushes us out of the nest so we have to try and fly. But he flies alongside; and if our weak, unpracticed wings cause us to drop, he swoops under us. Catching us on his wings he carries us back to our nest, lets us rest awhile, and then nudges us out again.

However, we're not the only ones who have been reluctant to leave our cozy, secure nest. The disciples found being on the Mount of Transfiguration with Jesus and seeing Moses and Elijah so thrilling they wanted to stay there and make shelters. Instead Jesus led them down the mountain, back to the demanding crowds and all their miseries. Jesus wants to lead us there too. Even if we'd sometimes like to, we cannot remain five years old forever.

Thank you, Father, for times when you nudge me from the nest but then also cruise alongside to catch me when I fall.

Day 4   2 Tim. 2:15   "Who will prosper your work."

All This and Heaven Too?

Truth pushed to an extreme can become error. We see this illustrated in the promises of success, wealth, and health some preachers hold out to people today.

It is true that God does promise to lead and guide us in our decisions. He does promise to provide for our needs. And it is only fitting and right that we thank and praise God for the ways in which he has graciously "prospered our work." But he does not promise us the luxury of spiritual excitement and prosperity that some Americans preach.

Three serious flaws lie embedded in this philosophy.

First, the rewards are offered by these people as a motive for following Jesus. If material blessings do result, they are actually a byproduct.

Secondly, Scripture does not teach or support this "gospel" of success and wealth. Rather this philosophy has grown out of our modern culture.

Finally, this philosophy lacks universal validity; and the gospel, to be true gospel, must be equally valid for all people in all times in all places and in all situations. How can I go to the street people of Calcutta and say, "Follow Jesus, and you will have health, wealth, and success"?

When, I sometimes wonder, will all this flaky froth bubble away? When will we as God's people settle down to some serious, righteous, holy obedience?

O Christ, our suffering Savior, quench our fevered thirst of pleasure and stem our selfish greed of gain.

Day 5   Hab. 3:17-19   "All that is needful has been sent."

God Sends Faith

When rescue workers after three days dug him out from under the shattered ruins of Hiroshima, Noboru Iwamura wondered why he had been spared. Months of hospitalization and recovery followed before he was able to enter the university. There he met Jesus Christ and became a Christian. He also met a young woman survivor of Hiroshima, and they were married.

After receiving his medical degree, Dr. Iwamura began to care for the shunned lepers of Japan. Then he heard of the people of Nepal, most of them without any medical help. For five years he worked and saved until he and his wife had enough to buy equipment, supplies, and to care for their own needs. Off to Nepal they went.

Childless because of radiation, they still longed to have children. So they adopted first one orphan, then another and another, including one blind and one physically handicapped. When leukemia made it no longer advisable to stay on in Nepal where risk of infection is great, they returned to Japan.

When I met Dr. Iwamura in 1980 in Kobe, he said, "Normally I shouldn't be able to continue to live, but I am trusting God daily to keep me alive until all 12 of our children have been educated and are able to care for themselves." His face radiated joy. "God has been so good," he said.

I thought of the marvel of God's grace that this man and woman had been able to live out what they believed, that "all that is needful" had been "sent by [God's] gracious ordaining." Had God sent the destruction of their health? No. Their inability to bear children? No. But he sent the will, courage, determination, and ability to trust God to surmount all this, and in joy pour out their lives in selfless service to God and others.

Help me trust you through all the difficulties that enter my life, O God.

Day 6   2 Cor. 9:7   "O let all that is in me adore him."

Expressing Your Gratitude

A few years ago my husband and I returned to Mount Kilimanjaro where our family had lived for eight and one-half years while our children were young. Walking down a road on a Sunday afternoon we met a choir. The women were all decked out in their brightly colored wrap-arounds and head turbans. As they came walking toward us, we heard them singing. Where had they been? we asked when we met. Visiting the sick and shut-ins, they said.

Ah, yes, we understood. For during the years we had lived with the Chaggas, we had discovered the many ways they let praise and adoration burst from their hearts. They sang *The Messiah* at Christmas, and caroled all night long Christmas Eve. When guests visited us, they sometimes would come and sing outside our house in praise to God for bringing fellow Christians to their midst.

They practiced other forms of praise also. If a student had passed an examination, if a family member had recovered from illness, if a crop had yielded a good harvest, if a birthday was being celebrated, they would bring an offering of bananas, coffee, chickens, or a goat to church on Sunday morning.

Once my husband gave a ride to an old man who was trying to walk slowly home after a visit to the clinic. The next morning a huge bunch of bananas appeared at our door. "You can never outgive a Chagga," we used to say.

Paul wrote about the rich generosity of the Christians in Macedonia. They themselves, though extremely poor and suffering, were so filled with joy that their joy had to overflow in giving, not only as they were able, but beyond their ability (2 Cor. 8:1-7).

"O let all that is in me adore him!" How much more cheerful and contented all of us would be if we would find more ways to give expression to our thanksgiving and praise to God.

Forgive me when I am stingy in praising you, O God.

Week 17

Jesus, Savior, Pilot Me

Edward Hopper, 1818–1888
John E. Gould, 1822–1875

1 Je - sus, Sav - ior, pi - lot me O - ver life's tem - pes - tuous sea; Un - known waves be - fore me roll, Hid - ing rock and treach - 'rous shoal; Chart and com - pass come from thee. Je - sus, Sav - ior, pi - lot me.

2 As a moth - er stills her child, Thou canst hush the o - cean wild; Bois - t'rous waves o - bey thy will When thou say'st to them: "Be still." Won - drous sov - 'reign of the sea, Je - sus, Sav - ior, pi - lot me.

3 When at last I near the shore, And the fear - ful break - ers roar Twixt me and the peace - ful rest, Then, while lean - ing on thy breast, May I hear thee say to me: "Fear not, I will pi - lot thee."

Day 1   Col. 3:15-17   "Jesus, Savior, pilot me."

A God Not Only for Sundays

Edward Hopper, author of this hymn, served as pastor of the Church of Sea and Land in New York harbor for many years. Sailors from ships at dock would wander into his church. Hopper wondered how he could better appeal to them. He decided to write a hymn about the life they knew best—life at sea. In doing so Hopper was following the lead of Luther who always sought to make the Bible of practical value by applying it to the life situations of his people. He drew from events of the day and everyday experiences of people for illustrations. Since one spends most of one's life at work, Luther thought God should be most real in that situation.

David, a Christian who is property manager of 19 apartment buildings, agrees. David hires managers, painters, and repairmen, and visits tenants who are delinquent in rents. "I first take care of business," he says. "Then I close my books and witness. I have had the joy of praying with many to receive Christ and then referring them to a Christian fellowship. My work also brings me into homes torn with strife and anguish because of marital problems or because of children in trouble through drugs or drinking. I have been surprised how often people are open to listen to a word of witness about Jesus. I try to direct them to a church close to their home for more help."

Hopper, using a familiar metaphor in his hymn, sought to show sailors how they could trust God for all they encountered in their daily work. Because David is part of the daily lives of his clients he learns of their heartaches, and is able to minister to them.

Quite possibly you too better understand the everyday life of those with whom you work than does your pastor. You can understand and speak the language of your colleagues. Your place of work can become a place of witness and ministry for you too.

Help me, Lord, to have open eyes, ears, and heart every day I work.

Day 2   Ps. 107:23-30   "Over life's tempestuous sea."

Life Can Be Rough

We set off, brave and confident in our little steel ship that is solidly riveted and welded, able to sail any sea—we think. The going is smooth to begin with. We cruise through the tranquil seas and glory in crashing through white-capped breakers when they appear. Then suddenly something rips through the side of our little ship in the form of disease, accident, divorce, a child on drugs, a home crumbled by an earthquake, or a farm lost through bankruptcy. In the horrifying hours that follow, we discover our little steel ship is really only a fragile paper boat tossed about on the waves, and we are out of control.

We also discover that the advertising world has deluded us into believing we have a right to expect from life that which life cannot guarantee us. "You deserve the best." "Treat yourself." This is what we are told repeatedly. But if we really deserve the best, why aren't we getting it? And why don't we have the resources to treat ourselves whenever we want to?

Slowly it becomes more and more real to us that we live in a world broken by sin. Because of this brokenness we can expect pain, heartache, disappointment, disloyalty, cruelty, suffering, and death. "I guess it's my turn now," may be the more appropriate response to make when trouble strikes. Life is a tempestuous sea. Our vessel is frail. We can expect to be tossed about. But we need not ride out the storm alone. "Jesus! Jesus, Savior!" we can call out. "Be my pilot. Steer my boat. Bring me safe to harbor." And he will.

> "One trouble calls another on
>   And gathers overhead,
> Falls splashing down, till round my soul
>   A rising sea is spread.
> Why restless, why cast down, my soul?
>   Hope still, and you shall sing
> The praise of him who is your God,
>   Your health's eternal spring.
>   Nahum Tate

Day 3   Ps. 102:1-11   "Unknown waves before me roll."

A Line Fine and Precarious

I write these words as a dear friend is undergoing brain surgery. She has been in the operating room five hours already. We, a handful of family and friends, are keeping vigil. She has stubbornly fought cancer for three years. It went into hiding for a while, fooled us into thinking it was gone, and now the beast has shown up again, crouched in the back of her brain. What will the outcome of the surgery be? Who knows? We don't yet. Nor do the doctors. We know there couldn't be a more dangerous place for the cancer to imbed itself, for that area controls the vital organs of the body. Will she come back from surgery blind? Will her kidney and liver function? Will she be able to walk? Talk? Remember? Or most terrifying of all: will she come back alive?

Of course we keep hoping for the best. Maybe the tumor isn't as large as we thought. Maybe that dark spot on the CAT Scan indicated mostly fluid. Maybe they can get all the malignancy. Maybe it isn't even malignant. Maybe God will work a miracle. Maybe, maybe, maybe. The unknown.

I remember what Jeanne Crumley wrote after her battle with cancer: "I have realized now that we all tread a fine and precarious line in our lives as human beings. Mine is no finer now than it was before, nor is my situation radically different from anyone else's. It's rather that I realize all this now."

What a gracious gift this realization is! It bequeaths us the wisdom we need to make necessary arrangements. It teaches us to find our security in God and to value courage.

When terrifying times of crisis come and our bodies go numb and our minds are unable to think rationally, stand by our sides, O God. Help us to entrust our future, our loved ones, and ourselves to you.

(A year later: My friend lived, and although life is not what it was before, she walks and talks and no trace of cancer has been found in her body. However, life continues to call for daily courage and faith.)

Day 4   Isa. 7:1-14   "Hiding rock and treach'rous shoal."

Pain Hunts False Faith

A pastor whose child had died from cancer said bitterly, "People talk about how testings like this can strengthen faith. Maybe it does for some. But I've seen it shatter the faith of some in our congregation. Nothing I say will bring them back to church."

George Macdonald, in *Diary of an Old Soul*, wrote of what can happen when faith is tested:

> The heaven is black with cloud and coming rain,
> High soaring, faith is grown a heavy task,
> And all is wrong with weary heart and brain.
> "Things do go wrong. I know grief, pain, and fear.
> I see them lord it sore and wind around."
> From her fair twilight answers Truth, star-crowned,
> "Things wrong are needful where wrong things abound.
> Things go not wrong, but Pain, with dog and spear
> False faith from human hearts will hunt and hound.
> The earth shall quake 'neath them that trust the solid ground" (Augsburg, 1965).

The questioning and doubting that come when troubles strike us are some of the sharp rocks and shallow shoals that lie hidden, ready to pierce our boats or run them aground. It is when we're hurting or stranded that we discover what has been only pretend faith on our part or what is real faith. Pretend faith is simply verbalizing statements we have been taught. Real faith is what we believe enough to act on.

"I think of it in this way," a young friend said. "Jesus is at the wheel of a motor boat. He invites me to ride the water skis behind his boat. I trust him enough to get on those skis. I trust him to maintain the right speed to keep me afloat, to execute curves correctly, and to avoid treacherous places. And if it happens that I fall, I trust him to come alongside and haul me out, so we can take off again." That's faith.

O Lord, surrounded by all the uncertainties of life, may we trust you enough to let you be in charge of our lives.

Day 5   Isa. 42:16; 58:11   "Chart and compass come from thee."

God Knows the Way

When God called him to leave the familiar and venture into a future about which he knew nothing, what gave Abraham courage to set out? It was God's promise: "Go to the land *that I will show you.*" It was the confidence he had that God would lead him. Abraham had tents made and, gathering together what was needed, he set off. The tents, probably made of sewn-together black goat hides, were a constant reminder to Abraham of the transitoriness of life. The altars he erected spoke to him of the presence of God.

Knowing the chart and compass for our lives are in God's hands is never more comforting and reassuring than when some trouble impresses on us the unpredictability, uncertainty, and transitoriness of life. The Bible reverberates with God's promises that he will guide us.

This promise of his guidance God gives, not only to people in general, but to each of us in particular. Before I went to India, Africa, and Singapore those places, in my thinking, contained only nameless masses of people. But now, having lived there, when I hear the names, my mind's eye brings into focus certain loved individuals. Thus God always sees, not the masses but individuals. And his vision is not limited like mine. He sees and knows and cares for *every* person in India, Africa, and Singapore—staggering though that thought is—and he offers his guidance to each one. "He leads *me,*" the psalmist David wrote. Indeed he does and will. Jesus has the chart and compass for me. He knows the way he is taking me. I can trust him. He will safely steer my little boat.

Lord, when change shatters my life that was so comfortable and secure before, help me keep my eyes in trust on you, you who are the never-changing One in your love and care and concern for me.

Day 6   John 19:25-27   "When at last I near the shore."

What About My Family?

Richard Byrd, alone in a hut in the Antarctic, wrote of his close encounter with death. "I felt myself sinking . . . death was a stranger sitting in a darkened room, secure in the knowledge that he would be there when I was gone. Great waves of fear, a fear I had never known before, swept through me and settled deep within. But it wasn't the fear of suffering or even of death itself. It was a terrible anxiety over the consequences to those at home if I failed to return" (*Triumph Over Odds,* Ed. J. Donald Adams, Duell, Sloan and Pierce, 1957).

Anxiety for loved ones who will be left behind is a real fear for those who are seriously ill. While certain steps can and should be taken to put business affairs in order, we wonder if our loved ones will have emotional stamina to cope and carry on. To alleviate these fears too we need to hear Jesus say, "Do not fear." God will enable our loved ones to carry on. Remember how he encouraged young Joshua after Moses died? "As I was with Moses, so I will be with you; I will never leave you nor forsake you" (Josh. 1:5). And Joshua not only survived, but carried on nobly and courageously.

As the hymn writer points to a solution for our troubled anxieties, he returns to the simile of a mother. He knows nothing brings more comfort or peace to a crying child than to be picked up by a loving mother and held close. So he writes, "then, while leaning on thy breast, May I hear Thee say to me: 'Fear not, I will pilot thee.' " But he also goes beyond the help a mother can give. "Wondrous Sov'reign of the sea!" he cries. Sovereign One. God Most High. The God who is above all. Who has control over the storms that threaten our fragile boats. "Jesus, Savior, pilot me!"

It's a cry God always hears. He comes, he puts his arms around and under us, and we are safe.

Understanding, faithful God, enable me to entrust my loved ones to your care, believing that those who do not trust you will be led to faith and that those who do will become stronger Christians in every way.

Day 1   Isa. 43:14-19   "Have we trials?"

When Life Slides from under Us

Joseph Scriven, the author of this hymn, suffered greatly. In his early 20s, on the eve of his wedding, his fiancée accidentally drowned. Plunged in grief and suffering from depression, he emigrated to Canada. A bachelor of arts degree, earned earlier at Trinity College in the United Kingdom, qualified him to teach, and to this he turned his attention. Teaching, however, had not been his first choice of a career. Joseph had hoped to join his father who was a captain in the Royal Marines, but ill health had ruled this out.

Joy and hope trickled into his life when he met Eliza Roche, but quickly evaporated when Eliza became violently ill and died.

Scriven knew no other place to which to turn for solace than the Scriptures. As he studied the Sermon on the Mount, he felt he should obey it literally. He began to give away all he had and gave his time to caring for the sick and poor. His health deteriorated. He worried about becoming a financial burden to others. Periods of depression grew more frequent and severe. On October 10, 1866, the townspeople of Rice Lake learned Scriven had drowned in the lake. Accidental or not? No one knew.

Tragic though his life was, Scriven let his suffering find a creative outlet when he penned the hymn, "What a Friend We Have in Jesus." He sent it to his mother in Ireland to comfort her at a time of sorrow. After her death, friends found it at her bedside and published it.

Although most of us do not suffer to the extent Scriven did, sooner or later suffering, in one form or another, will enter our lives. When this happens we too can seek to let our sorrow work itself out in creative expressions, all the way from gardening, to joining a support group for the suffering, to devoting ourselves to art or literary work, to opening our home to the lonely—the ways are unlimited. But as we shift our focus from ourselves to others, our sorrow will become a redemptive force in our lives and bring joy to others.

O God, may our sorrows find creative expressions.

Day 2   Psalm 88   "You will find a solace there."

Dark Seas of Depression

How much unuttered suffering did Scriven endure before that night when the wine-dark, cold waters of the lake silently closed over him? After his multiple tragedies did people withdraw from him? Not because they didn't care, but maybe because they just didn't know what to say. Others simply had their own calendars to pay attention to. Did Scriven misinterpret their withdrawal? Lonely people sometimes do. "Do your friends despise, forsake you?" he asks, but then counsels, "Take it to the Lord in prayer." Surely Scriven sought to do this. What then went wrong?

We need to understand that serious depression needs to be treated. Lillian and Raymond Grissen wrote about Lillian's three and one-half years of hospitalization for depression in *Toward Understanding Depression* (CRC Publications). Lillian said her Bible only condemned her. "Put it away," her doctor advised. "You don't know how to use it just now." Having friends tell her to cheer up didn't help. Lillian's pastor, however, helped as he continued faithfully to visit her. "I can't even pray," Lillian sobbed one day. "That's all right," her pastor comforted her, "because *we're* all praying for you."

For Raymond, the most meaningful help came when friends said, "We'll take the baby, we'll care for the other three children."

Do you know someone who is depressed? Can you encourage them to express their true feelings to you? Ask tactful questions that will provide them opportunities to talk about what is bothering them and then *listen*. Love them with warmth, but not with a possessive love. Affirm them. Help them see themselves as persons of inestimable value, at the same time as you encourage them to accept their humanity and their limitations. Remind them that this side of eternity God doesn't expect them to be perfect, but he does love them. And if their depression appears serious, see that they get skilled help.

Gift me, O God, with compassion, sensitivity, and wisdom.

Day 3   Lam. 3:22-25   "Are you weak and heavy laden?"

Giving Our Needs to Jesus

The dreary days of the Depression of the 1930s grew even more dreary for 32-year-old Margaret when her husband died, leaving her with three small children and two aging parents to care for. Margaret turned to the Lord for help.

Someone told her of a position open for work during the night. Determined to keep her family together and provide for them, Margaret took the job. "To pray is to work," she said.

But the days and nights took their toll. Bereavement alone brought exhaustion. Added to that was anxiety over the future. The few hours she had to sleep were broken and troubled. Many times Margaret wondered how much longer she could carry on. Again and again she turned to the Lord.

In the meantime Margaret's determination had deeply impressed the officers of the bank where she was making mortgage payments for her home. They called her to come for an interview.

If she would be willing to move, they said, they would make it possible for her to shift to a duplex. The duplex would cost no more than her present home and her monthly payments would not increase. She and her family could live in one portion of the duplex and rent out the other half to cover the cost of her monthly payments. Gratefully Margaret accepted their offer.

Years later Margaret said that, as far as she knew, the bank made that kind of an offer to no one else. "I had come to the place where I was wondering how I could go on," she said. "I cried to the Lord again in my helplessness, and I can only conclude that what happened was God working on my behalf."

"Helplessness is the attitude of heart which God recognizes as prayer," O. Hallesby wrote in *Prayer*. "To pray is to open our heart's door to Jesus. This is only a question of our wills. Will we give Jesus access to our needs? All he needs is access. He desires to come in and will enter wherever he is not denied admittance" (Augsburg, 1959).

What are your present needs? Spend some time talking to the Lord about this.

Day 4   2 Cor. 12:7-10   "What peace we often forfeit."

Prayer That Brings Peace

During my years in India Sundays closed as they began—in church. Often only a handful gathered for the English service. Nevertheless, Rev. Duncan conducted the service with careful preparation and dignity. Now, years later, I remember more than anything else his pastoral prayers. He prayed confidently and quietly as he embraced peoples near and far in all kinds of situations.

Sometimes he would join us on Saturday nights when a dozen of us would gather in the upstairs room of a Nepali home right in the heart of the marketplace. He would kneel slowly and carefully, his stiff bones creaking. I used to feel sorry for him, wondering how much the warped, wooden floorboards were hurting his bony, 70-year-old knees. But if he was uncomfortable, he never showed it. Instead he prayed—prayed fervently that God would open the closed land of Nepal so the Bible could be brought in. Though he prayed with passion, still it was with that same peaceful, confident, relaxed attitude. It impressed me. As I listened more carefully, I began to hear how frequently he ended his requests with, "If it glorify you, O Lord." And I began to understand the source of his peace. Praying for him was not dictating to God. Praying was seeking that which would bring glory to God.

For Jesus this too was true. Praying, "Your will be done," brought peace to Jesus and courage for the pain and suffering that lay ahead. Paul had to learn to pray that prayer when he was praying that his "thorn" be removed. In recent years, a woman with an incurable disease who for years had basked in a sense of God's presence, suddenly felt abandoned by him. "I am praying," she wrote, "that I won't yield to the temptation of talking about his presence when I feel only his absence, but rather will be enabled to accept his absence and glorify him in this testing too."

We forfeit peace when we do not pray, "if your name is glorified."

"May you be glorified!" Teach me to pray that prayer, O God.

Day 5   Isa. 53:1-6   "*All* our . . . griefs to bear."

He Shoulders Our Burdens

A stroke had felled my mother, paralyzing her. Mary, her oldest granddaughter, sat by her bedside holding her hand.

"I'm no good any more, Mary," Mother sobbed, the tears running down her cheeks. "I'm not good for anything."

"You may feel that way, Grandma, but I'm sure others don't," Mary comforted.

Sickness brings a sense of loss. It is significant that the words in Isa. 53:4 can be translated either as "infirmities," "sicknesses," "griefs," "sorrows," or "pain." When Matthew quotes this verse in Matt. 8:17, he sees it as a prophetic utterance fulfilled when Jesus healed the sick.

But Jesus bore not only our sicknesses and the grief and sorrow that accompanies sickness. He also took up and carried all our sorrows. "He was . . . a man of sorrows and familiar with suffering," Isaiah declared (53:3). *Familiar* would indicate that he had occasions frequently to grieve.

No sorrow, no grief can come to us that Jesus has not borne. He knows how we suffer. Loss of a loved one, health, a limb, job, or possessions; the disappointments we experience; the dreams unrealized; the hurts of having children ignore or disappoint us; of suffering unjustly; of being misunderstood; of having love betrayed—there is no grief, no sorrow that Jesus does not understand. You can bring them all to him. He will help you bear them. You may have a burden, but you also have shoulders. "Take my yoke upon you," Jesus said. Put your shoulder under the yoke of suffering or grief. Then let Jesus slip his strong shoulder under the other end of the yoke and bear it with you. By allowing you to bear the yoke with him, he may not take your suffering from you, and you may still continue to grieve. But in carrying your burden with you, Jesus will give you strength. And in calling forth from you courage, patience, and trust you did not know were possible before, God will be giving you an even more gracious gift than he would by relieving you entirely of your burden. Allow him to do so. He is waiting for you.

Thank you, Jesus, for putting your shoulder under my burden.

Day 6   Phil. 1:3-11; 4:1   "What a friend we have in Jesus."

Friends Help Us Know Jesus

Moses spoke face to face with God as a man speaks with his friend. Abraham is referred to as the friend of God. But, it appears, in Old Testament times few people other than Moses and Abraham learned to know God in this first-hand way. Most of the children of Israel had to learn and trust him through his providential acts, his Word, and through interaction with each other.

We who know the New Testament fare better. Christ revealed God to us so clearly that we can have confidence in God's immeasurable, redeeming love. Still for many of us, we first see the love of Christ in each other, and then we are able to trust Christ himself, and trust is the prelude to establishing any friendship, even with Jesus.

Probably because each of us so imperfectly and inadequately portrays Christ, God gives us a number of friends. From each of them we learn different facets of God's character, his tenderness, kindness, patience, humility, love, long-suffering, sympathy, creativity, generosity, industry, courage, and more.

We need many friends to help us learn to trust God. What one lacks, another can make up. Together they can all help us know and trust Jesus as our friend.

How blessed I am! I think of scattered, tiny groups of two, three, five, and six Christians in remote countries hostile to Christianity. How cut off they are from the strengthening, life-imparting, trust-building communion of saints! Let none of us ever take this gift of grace for granted, but thank God for it every day. Without it, our knowledge and experience of Jesus as our friend would not be as rich as it is.

Take a few moments and review the particular Christian characteristics you see reflected in each of your friends. How have your friends helped you come to know and trust Jesus as the best friend of all?

Thank you, God, for my Christian friends.

Week 19

For the Beauty of the Earth

Folliott S. Pierpoint, 1835–1917, alt.
Conrad Kocher, 1786–1872

1 For the beau-ty of the earth, For the beau-ty of the skies,
2 For the won-der of each hour Of the day and of the night,
3 For the joy of ear and eye, For the heart and mind's de-light,
4 For the joy of hu-man love, Broth-er, sis-ter, par-ent, child,

For the love which from our birth O-ver and a-round us lies:
Hill and vale and tree and flow'r, Sun and moon and stars of light:
For the mys-tic har-mo-ny Link-ing sense to sound and sight:
Friends on earth and friends a-bove; For all gen-tle thoughts and mild:

Refrain
Christ, our Lord, to you we raise This our sac-ri-fice of praise.

5 For yourself, best gift divine   Agent of God's grand design,
    To the world so freely giv'n;   Peace on earth and joy in heav'n: *Refrain*

Day 1   Ps. 24:1-2   "For the beauty of the earth."

Caring for Our Earth

This morning I read Annie Dillard's Pulitzer Prize-winning essay, "The Fixed" from *Pilgrim at Tinker Creek*. Annie takes me with her on her nose-reddening, nose-dripping February walks along Corvin's Creek in search of praying mantis egg cases. When we find them, we will carefully carry home the branches to which they are affixed so we can tie them to branches of trees in our garden. Why? So in June when the praying mantis hatches, it will gobble up destructive insects and then "clean its smooth green face like a cat."

I wish I had a Corvin's Creek where I could find praying mantis egg cases, but I live in a cement megapolis. So I will have to find some less natural way to help my flowers grow. But I worry about how the pesticides we are using pollute the air.

Caring for our earth home isn't easy. Even too much water unnaturally poured on the ground can be harmful. Some farmers here in California say they have irrigated so often the soil has become too saline to bear crops. Our craze to make the earth and all that populates it produce more and more also threatens. When our daughter was expecting, though she needed the iron, she didn't dare eat liver more than once a month because of the steroids fed to animals to make them larger and heavier.

Some time ago when we visited India, I wondered how long we would have to travel until we reached the Terai, the plains area bordering the southern boundary of Nepal. From years past I remembered this area as being heavily forested. When we came to a spot where the majestic, ancient trees lay felled, I understood that the Terai as I had known it, existed no more. As we traveled up the mountain slopes of Nepal, we saw they too had been stripped of trees and were eroding. "Nepal's chief export to India is topsoil," a man said to me sadly.

"This is my Father's world," we sing in a hymn. Indeed it is, and he created it picture book pretty and would have it stay that way. But for us, the big question is: how can we be better keepers and tenders of our world?

O Creator God, make us willing to be wise tenders of the earth.

Day 2   Exod. 13:21   "For the beauty of the skies."

The Cloud with a Name

Many years ago there was a cloud named Shekinah. Shekinah was unusual not only in that it had more than a family name, but Shekinah was different in other respects also. Although it was funnel-shaped like a tornado, it was not dark and menacing, but glowed with a molten light so vibrant that seen against the pitchy darkness of night, some thought the cloud had caught fire. Another unusual feature of Shekinah was its constancy. It didn't go leaping, skipping, and chasing across the skies like tornado clouds do. Nor did it drift lazily along like the cumulus clouds. Instead neither Shekinah's form nor its position in the heavens changed. The only time Shekinah moved was when God commanded it to move, for God had given Shekinah to the Israelites for a special purpose. Shekinah, in the first place, was to be a visible sign to the children of Israel of God's constant presence with them. It embodied the glory of God—which is what Shekinah refers to—so that when people entered the tabernacle over which Shekinah hovered, the awesome glory of God immediately gripped them, and they would fall on their faces in worship.

God had also told the children of Israel that he would guide them by the movements of Shekinah. Whenever Shekinah lifted and began to move, they were to pack up their belongings, take down their tents, roll them up and set off, following the cloud. But if the cloud did not lift, they were not to make any move.

Shekinah also protected God's people. When the Egyptians pursued the Israelites, the cloud moved between the two armies, casting a shadow over the Egyptians so dark they couldn't see the Israelites.

Though Shekinah disappeared once the Israelites were settled in Israel, it reappeared again other times, as when it enveloped God's Son on the Mount of Transfiguration (Matt. 17:5).

No Shekinah hangs in the heavens for us to see today, but we may let the clouds in the sky remind us of God's constant presence with us, too, to guide and protect us.

Thank you, Lord, for the promise of your constant presence with us.

Day 3   Matt. 6:25-34   "For the wonder of each hour."

Mrs. What-If Lady

Once upon a time there lived a lady whose name was What-If Lady. That wasn't her real name actually, but that is what her neighbors called her, for she was always saying, "What if?"

For example, her husband moved their family into a two-story house so they and their children could have plenty of room. Mrs. What-If Lady said, "But what if an earthquake comes while we're downstairs and the whole upstairs falls on top of us?"

When Mrs. What-If Lady went to a party, she always said, "What if I can't sleep if I eat all this rich food?" and so she never ate a thing.

When her husband called in a plumber, Mrs. What-If Lady lay awake the night before he came. "What if the plumber he called doesn't know his job?" she worried.

And so dear Mrs. What-If Lady wasted a great deal of her energy worrying about needless what-ifs and was unable to enter into the joy and wonder of each hour of the day and of the night.

Jesus gently and lovingly chided those who had slipped into what-iffing. If God gave you life, will he not care for you also? he asked. Don't miss enjoying the radiant beauty of the scarlet poppies even if they bloom for only one day and then are gathered up with the weeds, dried, and tossed into clay ovens to get the fires going. Enjoy them while they bloom.

Jesus tells you not to let worry over the harvest prevent you from absorbing all the joy summer offers. Not to let anxiety about how your kids will turn out keep you from enjoying them now. Not to be so apprehensive about the last days and years of your life that you can't live fully now. He taught that worrying isn't going to change a thing except you might get ulcers. And if some of the things you dread so much actually do happen, remember, he'll be there to help you through those wearisome times too.

Faithful Father God, give me pleasure in life today. And if pleasure is too much to ask because some of the things I had never wanted to happen to me have happened, then help me to be undaunted and undismayed.

Day 4   Ps. 66:8-12   "For the wonder . . . of the night."

When It's Difficult to Praise

What wonder can be found in hours described by one dying of cancer? "What I have experienced during the late night and early morning hours has been white-hot and totally overpowering," she wrote.

Or what occasion for praise is there when for a 55-year-old wife, the hours of a day hold only trips to a health center to color children's coloring books and play bean bags with her husband, a victim of Alzheimer's disease?

And yet . . . and yet the wonder is there, discovered by many who suffer thus.

The wonder, as George Macdonald expressed it, is that when "all things seem rushing straight into the dark," God enables us to believe he is there in the dark with us.

The wonder is that when minutes drip like hours, God gives us courage, strength, and patience.

It is the wonder that four walls, shutting us in, need not make us prisoners. "One area has been enhanced rather than curtailed for me," writes a 76-year-old shut-in, crippled with arthritis and racked with coughing spells, "and that is the privilege of intercession through which I can support those who are fit enough to be active."

The wonder is that when God gives us a task too big for hands that have done only little things, then what we cannot do, God will do through us the thing that is too big for us.

For the miraculous, grace-filled wonder of these hours, we can thank and praise God.

Spend some time in prayer and praise, thanking God for difficult times when God stayed by your side, sustaining you and bringing you through.

Day 5   Isa. 35:3-7   "For the joy of ear."

Let the Birds Sing

Transplanted Chinese in the city-state of Singapore compensate partly for the countryside sounds they miss hearing by keeping birds as pets. In the evening or on Saturday afternoons or Sundays the men will frequently carry their birds in their cages to a park, hang the cages from a branch of a tree, and then sit down underneath to listen to the concert.

A young African student studying here in the States wrote in a little book, *I Sing Your Praises All the Day Long:* "Lord, I am homesick for Africa where the first noise is not an alarm clock, but father's voice saying, 'Let us pray' " (Friendship Press, 1970).

What sounds would you miss most if you suddenly were deprived of your hearing? Take a few minutes and make a list.

People who cannot hear suffer, and most often do so silently. After Jane Merchant, the renowned Tennessee invalid poet of the 1940s through the 1960s lost her hearing, she communicated mainly by writing. But on holidays when the extended family gathered to celebrate, it was easy for the family to forget to take time to include Jane in their merriment by writing. Lying in her bed, observing the happy facial expressions and the chattering, Jane would feel very lonely.

"My David," a friend wrote, referring to her husband, "is losing his hearing. He is feeling the isolation and withdrawing more and more."

If Jesus' ministry of love and caring included those who could not hear—and it did (Mark 7:32)—should not we also care and ask ourselves what we can do to include those who feel shut out of the activities of life?

For the gift of hearing which I so often take for granted, thank you, Lord. Forgive me when I am not sensitive to the need to be included of those who cannot hear well. Save me from telling jokes that make fun of disabilities. Help me understand how I, in some small way, can help meet the needs people have, needs about which they say so little.

Day 6   Prov. 18:24   "For the joy of . . . friends."

Friends

A mother was playing with her little daughter. "What does the dog say? The cat? The duck?" Then the mother asked, "What does your Daddy say?" The little girl's face lit up. "Daddy says, 'I love you!' " she exclaimed.

Unfortunately, Jonathan, the "poor little rich boy" we read about in the Old Testament, wasn't as sure of his father's love as the little girl was of hers. Jonathan, the son of a king, had grown up with every need, every want supplied. That is, every need except love from his father. Saul didn't know how to love. In the first place, his inferiority complex that had led him to put on a show of bravado, caused him to act independently of God. When he failed, he wouldn't take responsibility but blamed others. He lied and was defensive when others criticized him. To compensate for his feelings of insecurity, he sought to build up the power of his army. Most serious, he was fickle in his closest relationships. He allowed jealousy and suspicion to poison him and began to hate as fiercely as he once had loved. With all these negative qualities, Saul was incapable of giving Jonathan the love he needed.

So Jonathan turned to David for friendship, and the hearts of the two were knit together, and a relationship forged that survived crisis after crisis.

Family, when it functions as it was meant to, should offer us a stable, secure, supportive oasis in our troubled world, an oasis to which we can always return, the place where we'll always be taken in, not because we deserve to be, but because we belong. Family ought to be the place where we can relax, where we don't have to be brave, and where we know we'll always be loved. Wealth, honors, and degrees should make no difference in families.

But families sometimes fail, and if our family cannot offer us the love and support we need, let us ask God to give us friends to make up the difference, even as we continue to pray for our own broken family.

For friends and family we thank you, O gracious God.

Week 20

The Church's One Foundation

Day 1   Acts 20:17-35   "One Lord, one faith, one birth."

Freeways to Nowhere

Speeding along the freeway in an unfamiliar area of the sprawling Los Angeles metropolis, I saw I was approaching a **Y** where two freeways would veer off in separate directions. Momentarily unsure, I wondered which one I should take. Then I saw the sign above one: "Freeway to Nowhere." It was an unfinished freeway, still under construction.

Throughout the ages cults have become freeways to nowhere for thousands. Lured to them by extravagant promises, people become so entangled, so mesmerized, and so deceived they cannot extricate themselves. When needs not met by the church burn and consume, people may turn to anyone who sets himself or herself in the position of a compassionate savior. In the beginning Jim Jones, moved by compassion, fed the hungry of Los Angeles, set up health clinics, and opened centers to teach reading. Perhaps, in the beginning, he himself did not intend to become the founder of a sadistic cult which ended in mass death.

Ever aware of the danger of the evil one leading people astray, faithful leaders of Christ's church have insisted on Christians receiving careful instruction in the articles of faith that summarize the Christian faith. Luther wrote a book of explanation for his children and used it also for his students.

Samuel John Stone, rector of an Anglican church in London and author of our hymn, wrote this hymn to sing the Third Article of the Apostles' Creed into the hearts and memories of his people. Dramas, quizzes, pictures, and art work also can plant deeply into the minds of our children the meaning of the Christian faith. Of course our lives also must reflect those teachings. But as we seek to do both, giving careful instruction to our children and following it ourselves, we shall have done what we could to save them from getting on freeways that lead to nowhere.

Establish us, our loved ones, and our church, O God, in the true faith.

Day 2   Rom. 12:15   "Yet one o'er all the earth."

We Belong to Each Other

Our youngest son had joined his brother and two sisters 300 miles away at boarding school. Their bedrooms now stood empty and always in order, and the house echoed with loneliness. The first Sunday in church I fought tears. I had not been home long when I heard the gate creak and looked out to see Judith, the wife of one of our African teachers, coming down the path. When she reached me, she grasped my hand and began to stroke my arm. "I saw your face in church this morning," she said, "and knew you were eating bitterness because your children are gone. I just want to say, 'I feel with you.'"

My eyes blurred. A year earlier I had held Judith in my arms as they had carried home from the hospital the dead body of her five-year-old son. My son would return. Hers wouldn't. Yet she was comforting me.

Koinonia is the Greek word for fellowship, that marvelous blending of spirits which Christians all over the world experience as they give to each other and receive in return. I had been able to comfort Judith. Now she was comforting me. Differences in ethnic and educational backgrounds, in cultural patterns and viewpoints about life all faded. We were simply two persons, bonded together by a common love: Christ's love for us, our love for him, and, because of this, our love for each other.

The early Christians experienced this "tie that binds." Paul introduced the Philippians to Christ. They provided for his material needs (Phil. 4:14-19). The Corinthians discovered that as they entered into Paul's sufferings, they, in turn, were comforted (2 Cor. 1:3-7).

Which do you think offers you the fullest opportunity for fellowship, for this communing of the saints: (1) a funeral, (2) participation in a drive for world hunger, (3) or an after-church coffee hour?

Teach us, O God, to share our mutual sorrows and troubles, to cry with one another and to comfort one another, rejoice with those who rejoice and mourn with those who mourn. May we empathize with one another and bear each other's burdens, and may "often for each other flow the sympathizing tear."

Day 3   Acts 2:42   "She is his new creation by . . . the Word."

How Does God Recreate Us?

Tom, who works as an attorney for a major corporation, admits enthusiasm for church has ebbed at times in his life. He participated as a youngster "primarily because my parents expected me to do so." When he attended a Christian college he went but only "out of a sense of duty."

But then several years later he enrolled in the Bethel Bible Series. "Studying the Old Testament helped me to know and understand a God who really loves us and is patient and forgiving even when we have been trying to direct our lives without him," Tom says.

At the same time he met people whose lives were motivated by Christ. "They weren't living for themselves but rather for others. Their openness impressed me. They emphasized they didn't have it all together, but were fellow strugglers."

Tom recognized that he was gaining something from studying with others that he would lose if he studied the Bible only by himself. To a significant degree we become what we are because of the ones with whom we associate. God makes us into new creations through his Word and through other Christians in whom that Word has taken on flesh and bones.

Dietrich Bonhoeffer, who was denied the companionship of other Christians during his years in prison, learned to value fellowship with other Christians deeply. "The physical presence of other Christians is a source of incomparable joy and strength to the believers," he wrote (*Life Together,* Harper and Row, Publishers, 1954).

We, who are not in prison, can rejoice in the gift that is ours to meet regularly for Sunday worship and Bible study with other Christians. Many of us who spend the majority of our time working with non-Christians can also meet with a few fellow Christians during our rest periods of work. Tom did. Others at his company heard about it and soon a number of small groups came into being. Once or twice a year at a prayer breakfast over 600 of them gather.

Teach me to be more truly thankful for all that is mine, O God.

Day 4   John 1:1-18   "The Church's one foundation."

River or Swamp

"Aren't all religions the same?" Has anyone ever asked you that question? A TV commentator once asked E. Stanley Jones, lifetime missionary to India, "What do you have to preach that others don't have?" Jones shot back the answer: "I have Jesus Christ—the Word become flesh" (E. Stanley Jones, *The Word Became Flesh*, Abingdon, 1963).

Jones went on to point out that other religions have words, but Christianity alone has the Word made visible among us for 33 years. As that Word (Jesus) moved among people, he called them to follow him. Not to follow a system of rules or thoughts, but to follow *him*.

"But have there not been many incarnations of God?" some asked Jones. "What about Mohammed, Krishna, Buddha, Confucius?" Jones replied, "Briefly, Vishnu himself had many incarnations: a boar, a tortoise, a fish, a dwarf, a man-lion, Rama, Krishna, Buddha. Rama, a warrior, was sinful; Krishna's character, shady. Buddha declared he did not believe in God. When you become liberal on essentials," Jones continued, "you become hazy."

In a day when the unique faith of Christianity often appears to be stated in indistinct and ambiguous terms, when the "in" thing is to accept everyone and every faith and to judge no one nor discern truth from error, we need to reaffirm loudly that the church's one foundation is Jesus Christ our Lord. Jesus Christ is the distinctive feature of Christianity. Jesus Christ, not merely a human, but God manifest in the flesh and bones of Jesus. Jesus dying on the cross to bear the consequences of our sins. Jesus rising from the dead and promising everlasting life after death to those who believe in him. None of the other religions will accept these declarations of faith. But if in our desire to be "broadminded," we depart from these affirmations of faith, we shall become shallow. "Maybe even a swamp," Jones said once. "The difference," he explained, "is a river has banks, while a swamp spreads over everything."

O faithful God, guard your church from becoming a swamp!

Day 5　　Matt. 26:26-29　　　　　　　　"Partakes one holy food."

The Meal We Eat Together

It was Easter, and they were in prison. Another prison held their wives. The streets of their city now knew their children as homeless waifs, wandering about, begging for food. Thomas G. Pettepiece, in his book, *Vision of a World Hungry* (The Upper Room, 1979) describes the experience of these political prisoners.

Faced with the possibility of their own imminent death, they had thought often of death and of friends who already were dead. Reading the Scriptures buoyed and steadied their faith and also reminded them of the followers of God who had died in faith. Now at Easter especially they longed to commune with Christ who had tasted of death for everyone and overcome it. Separated from loved ones, they yearned to know their companionship, even if only in a mystical way. "Let us celebrate the Lord's Supper," they said. "This is a meal we all have in common." But how? They had no bread, no cup. "Is God limited to earthly means?" they asked.

The men assembled. Pettepiece spoke the opening words, then asked each participant to extend an open palm. He cupped his own empty palm and placed it over the extended hand. "Take, eat, this is my body, given for you; do this in remembrance of me," he said. All raised their hands and "ate." Likewise with the wine. After a period of silent communion, they arose and embraced each other. Smiles mingled with tears. Hope shone on their faces. A non-Christian prisoner said, "You have something special I should like to have."

What does Holy Communion mean to us? How deeply have we learned to really commune and partake of Christ as we eat and drink? Can we also transcend earthly boundaries in yet another step of faith and experience "mystic sweet communion" also with those who have died in faith? Each time we commune, as we remember our Savior and his death and life, why can we not also remember a faithful believer who has died, and remembering that life of courage, faith, and sacrifice, be strengthened for our continuing journey?

Teach me to enter into communion with your saints, O Lord.

Day 6   Jer. 17: 7-8   "She is his new creation by . . . the Word."

God's Word Doesn't Speak to Me as It Used to Do. What Can I Do?

As Christians we believe God's Word has power to change us. Perhaps we also have known times when we actually were conscious of this happening. We saw some of our old distasteful habits being broken, and we were able, by God's grace, to discard them. We found ourselves worrying less and loving more. But now that seems changed. The Word doesn't seem to mean the same to us now. Maybe some of us, to remedy this, have joined Bible classes. We have studied the background, the times, the circumstances, the customs and the meaning of words. But still, reading the Word just doesn't mean what it once did. What can we do?

The best thing is to keep right on reading. Times of dryness pass. Growth can take place even when we are not aware of it. That is true of us physically. After the noticeable growth of childhood and the teen years, physical growth slows. But then one day we put on an old pair of trousers and discover the waist band is too tight or the trousers not long enough.

Now if physical growth sometimes takes place unnoticed, even more can this be true of spiritual growth. For example, one day we shall read a passage that has been obscure before and suddenly we shall understand it. Or some incident that previously would have upset us happens, and we find we react calmly. Growth has taken place.

Perhaps we also are working too hard at becoming a Christian. Maybe for a while we should focus on meditating. Sit in the presence of the Lord. Let your mind dwell on one word or phrase. Ask the Lord what he has to say to you. And if no "word" seems to come, relax. Thank him for all he means to you and all that is yours. Remember, he is the vine. Yours the task simply to abide, to rest in him. Then life will most surely flow through him to you.

And finally, start obeying more actively what you do understand the Bible telling you to be and do and watch what happens.

Dear God, help me commune with you as I read your word.

Week 21

O Master, Let Me Walk with You

Washington Gladden, 1836–1918
H. Percy Smith, 1825–1898

1. O Master, let me walk with you In lowly paths of service true; Tell me your secret; help me bear The strain of toil, the fret of care.
2. Help me the slow of heart to move By some clear, winning word of love; Teach me the wayward feet to stay, And guide them in the homeward way.
3. Teach me your patience; share with me A closer, dearer companying, In work that keeps faith sweet and strong, In trust that triumphs over wrong.
4. In hope that sends a shining ray Far down the future's broadening way, In peace that only you can give; With you, O Master, let me live.

149

Day 1 John 13:1-17 "In lowly paths of service true."

I'm Tired, Too

A. E. Whitman, in his book, *The Discipline and Culture of the Spiritual Life,* tells a parable in which a man, in his dreams, comes to a museum. He enters and the first thing he sees is some rusty old armor. But then his attention is distracted by the unusual collection in the next cabinet.

A little bird's feather. A piece of human hair. A coin. Some baby clothes. A hammer and nails. A sponge. Some thorn branches. A wine cup. When he sees 30 pieces of silver, he understands what he is seeing. As he stands reverently holding the wine goblet in his hands, he whispers to the attendant, "Have you got a towel and a basin too?" "No," the attendant shakes his head. "Not on display. You see, they're in constant use here."

When Jesus took the towel and basin to wash his disciples' feet, he was building on what had preceded that object lesson, for, in reality, that is what it was. Undoubtedly someone, the servant who had prepared the meal perhaps, already had washed the disciples' dusty feet when they arrived. Supper was over now. Their feet were clean. Then why wash them again? Luke tells us (Luke 22:24). Can't you hear them? Peter: "I'm the greatest. Jesus called me the rock." John: "Oh, come on! Didn't he ask me to sit next to him tonight?" Some made their own claims. Others cheered for their favorite. Jesus endured it for a while, and then got up and got busy. "Will you remember this in the future when you start quarreling about whose interests are the most important?" he was asking, in effect. For while, in one sense, the disciple is constantly to be using the towel and basin, other special times come too. Times to quit arguing: "My work at the office is most important!" "I'm tired too! Why do I have to help you?" Times to take up the towel, to do the dishes, to buy some groceries, walk the whining baby for a while. Jesus says that he'll do it. Will you?

It's hard to pick up the towel, Jesus. Help me.

Day 2   Col. 3:12-15   "Help me the slow of heart to move."

Not Just Getting a Tan

Janet, a seminary student, came to Singapore to take her Clinical Pastoral Education course which provides opportunities for pastoral experience in different settings, often in hospitals.

In the extended care unit Janet found a 55-year-old, well-educated man embittered because a stroke had paralyzed him. Previously he had held a high government position. Now, confined to a wheelchair and unable to care for himself, he felt life was meaningless.

The first morning Janet tried to talk with him, he used his one good hand to wheel himself away. The second morning he stayed, but did not grunt even one response. Finally Janet asked, "May I pray with you?" He nodded. But at the close, when she opened her eyes, she saw he had wheeled away.

Janet kept trying. One day she found him lying in the sun. His nurses hoped the sun would heal some of his sores. "They're barbequing me," he fumed.

Janet laid down on the ground beside him. The sun blazed down and Janet could feel perspiration breaking out on her arms and legs and her dress getting damp.

"Why are you lying here in the sun?" the man finally asked.

"Just wanted to see what things looked like from your viewpoint," Janet said. The man's face twitched. Little by little he began to pour out his grief; and when Janet asked if they could pray together, he readily agreed. The day Janet's internship was completed and she said good-bye to him, he wept.

Being willing to enter into the suffering of others enables them to open up and share their hurts. Can you think of someone who needs you to do this?

Give me the willingness to enter into the hurts of others, even if this means I will hurt, O compassionate Savior.

Day 3   Matt. 25:37-40   "Teach me the wayward feet to stay."

Too Fat to Move

A mother was talking on the phone to her daughter, Sue, who was at college. After the exchange of news, she asked, "Have you found a Bible class to attend on Sunday mornings?" Silence on Sue's end. "When Sue introduced another subject I was annoyed," the mother said. A few days later the phone rang. It was Sue. Sobbing. "Mom," she said, "Bill died." "Bill? Bill who?" the mother asked. "Haven't I told you?" Sue said. Then, interspersed with sobs, her story came out. Early in the school year on the way to church, Sue and a couple of her friends had noticed some men— evidently alcoholics—sitting dejectedly on benches in the park. The girls decided to cook a huge kettle of homemade soup and bring it to them every Sunday morning. Bill had the tremors so bad that Sue had to spoonfeed him. That morning she had come to the park and Bill was gone. She was absolutely heartbroken and cried for a long time. The mother concluded, "I can't tell you how I felt. Here I've been sitting in Bible class and church all these years getting fatter and fatter. It's no wonder I haven't been able to move to help someone."

"Haunts of wretchedness and need" exist in all our cities and now many of us live in cities. As far as possible we try to avoid even driving through those areas of need. "It's not safe," we say. No, it wasn't safe for Jesus either, moving about as he did. But if crossing those bridges seems totally impossible for us, how about neighbors, friends, relatives, companions at work who need to be rescued from their own pits of alcoholism, drug addiction, loneliness, despair, anger, and violence? They need to learn about Christ and his power to free them, but they may never know him if we don't do anything.

As Christians, we are called to witness to Christ but often we think only of words. Our words need to be accompanied by actions that show we care.

In "haunts of wretchedness and need, on shadowed thresholds dark with fears, from paths where hide the lures of greed" (Frank North), can we catch the vision of our Savior's tears?

Forgive me, Lord, when my commitment stops with mere words.

Day 4   Heb. 11:23   *"Teach me your patience."*

Is That Patience?

"Shh, don't let the baby cry! If a passing soldier hears him, that'll be the end. The neighbors know the child was born, but we can trust them—or at least we hope so. But not the police. Oh, my baby! I love you so, but I fear so for your life! These past months have made an old woman of me. We can't go on any longer this way. After a while you'll be talking and running around. We must think of something to do.

"I wonder if I hid your cradle in the reeds at the spot where the Pharaoh's daughter comes to bathe, what would happen? Can anyone with any heart at all resist an abandoned child? Oh, my baby, how I pray to the Lord that he will watch over you."

Patience, as it is used in the Bible, means much more than "endurance," though it carries that meaning too. A patient person is charged with faith and hope and expects something to happen. Moses' mother exhibited patience when she placed her baby in his basket in the river. Alfred Carlsen took his first trembling step in practicing patience when he picked up his little newborn baby daughter, wrapped her in a warm blanket and cuddled her. "We will thank God for this new life," he said to his wife who lay sobbing. "We will wrap our love around our little Anne and do everything we can to bring happiness to her." Inside that blanket lay a tiny one with only stumps for arms, six inches of thigh for one leg and a withered, twisted stump for the other.

"You can do it," Anne's father kept encouraging as Anne grew and faced each new situation, and he sought every means he could to make it possible. He provided her with artificial limbs, crutches, an education, and a spirit that despised self-pity but instead reached out to others. Today, in a school in Jamestown, North Dakota, that bears Anne Carlsen's name, other children with handicaps are learning both Anne's secret of courage and also how to become self-reliant. And it all began because her father understood and practiced biblical patience.

When my turn comes to exercise patience, give me wisdom to know what to do, O God.

Day 5   Phil. 4:4-13   "In work that keeps faith sweet and strong."

Joy Is a Happening

"Are you going to be a pastor like your father?" I asked a child. "Never!" was the reply. "It's much too boring."

Saddened, I thought of the joy we had seen on the faces of Mother Teresa's nuns the days we had spent with them. Sometimes we rode with them in their Landrover, combing the streets for the dying. Sometimes we walked with them from bed to bed as they lovingly cared for the sick and dying.

"You live with tragedy and death all the time," I said to one. "Yet your faces reflect joy. Tell me your secret."

"Every morning we arise early, first for a time of private prayer and reading of the Word," she began. "Then we come together to sing. We pray. Only after this do we begin our work. At noon we take a break, maybe to read a novel, or listen to music. In the evening we gather to thank God for his goodness and his promise that he will be with us on the morrow."

"Mother Teresa," she explained, "believes the poor and suffering are worthy of not only love, but a little joy, and if joy is to come to them, it must be Christ's joy, channeled through us. So we receive it from him first."

Like Mother Teresa's nuns, the early Christians knew how to sing as they worked. What was their secret? What set joy coursing in their hearts?

Christians applauded and celebrated when memorable events took place: when people came to faith in Christ, and were healed or freed from evil powers (Acts 8:7-8; 15:3). The Christians worked together as a team (2 Cor. 1:24); when one rejoiced, others rejoiced. They knew how to bring refreshment to each other (Philemon 7).

Joy, for the disciples and for Mother Teresa's nuns, was not something they *achieved* after struggling to attain it. Joy was something that *happened* when they did certain things. We can learn this secret too.

Help me understand, O God, that often joy and tragedy, pain and suffering walk hand in hand, and to be prepared for this.

Day 6   Heb. 11:39—12:2   "In hope that sends a shining ray."

He Didn't Give Up

Have you ever had so many ventures fail and so many things go wrong you've been tempted to give up? Some days are like that. We'd like to go back to bed and forget it all. And as we grow older and our bodies wear out, some days secretly we wish (we're not serious, of course) we could be an elderly Eskimo and just go outside, sit in the snow, and die there peacefully.

Well, we're not alone. We've lots of company.

But, hard as it is to believe, failures, as Edwin Markham wrote, can "shake the soul and let the glory out." Glory? How?

In demonstrations of determination, courage, and the refusal to give up.

I think of Ansgar, a missionary from the area we know today as Germany, who back in A.D. 826 had dreams that the Swedes would become Christians. But the rough, warlike Swedes had no interest in becoming peace lovers. Twice Ansgar tackled the job alone. Gleefully the Vikings attacked and robbed him. Ansgar didn't retreat immediately, and when he did, it was to call together others so a number could concentrate on the mission. Enraged, the Vikings swooped down on his sending base and burned the whole city of Hamburg.

Ansgar "kept on knocking." He tried the Danes. Things went no better. Ansgar finally died, his dreams unrealized. Though it was a barely perceptible crack that he had pushed the door open, still it was enough so later others could enter. And how about his shining example of not giving up? Of not letting defeat make him cynical or bitter or turning him into an unbeliever? Ah, we still remember that today. If Ansgar could persevere and die in faith, so can we! And we carry on.

There are days when I am tempted to give up, Lord. Rescue me on those days. Root out any self-pity that is trying to lodge within me. Help me say, "With God's help I can go on; I will go on."

Week 22

God Moves in a Mysterious Way

William Cowper, 1731–1800, alt.   Tans'ur, Compleat Melody, 1734

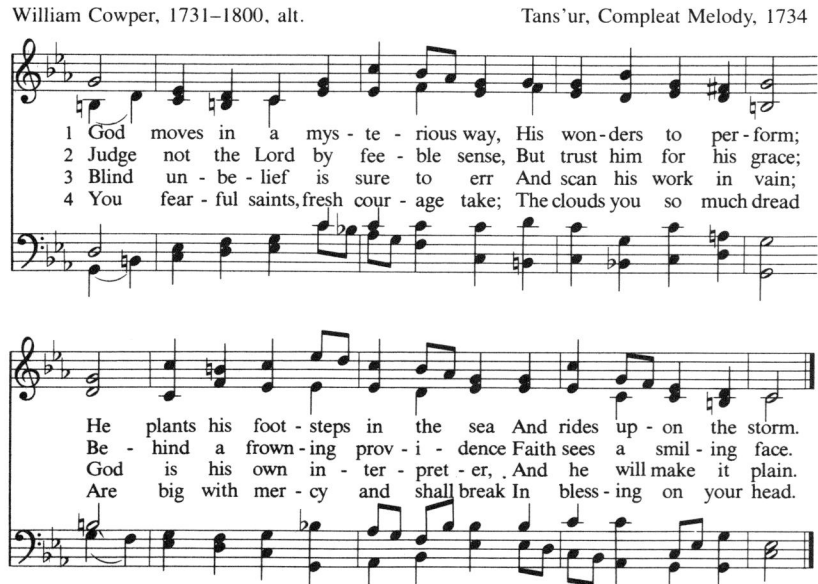

1 God moves in a mys-te-rious way, His won-ders to per-form;
2 Judge not the Lord by fee-ble sense, But trust him for his grace;
3 Blind un-be-lief is sure to err And scan his work in vain;
4 You fear-ful saints, fresh cour-age take; The clouds you so much dread

He plants his foot-steps in the sea And rides up-on the storm.
Be-hind a frown-ing prov-i-dence Faith sees a smil-ing face.
God is his own in-ter-pret-er, And he will make it plain.
Are big with mer-cy and shall break In bless-ing on your head.

Day 1   2 Cor. 12:7-10   "And rides upon the storm."

Suffering: Catalyst for Creativity

Life is beautiful, but life also withholds certain things from us, and so we suffer. Suffering is never good, but the way we respond to it can work for good in our lives and the lives of others. The choice is ours. In order for suffering to enrich our lives and ministry, we need to be enabled to accept it, to reflect on it, and to search for the meaning it holds for us and others. As we do this, deprivation can become the catalyst for creativity. We see this portrayed in the life of William Cowper.

Cowper's father was a pastor, but it was to his mother, a woman from a well-known family of royalty, that Cowper was deeply attached. She died when he was six, and his world crumbled.

Upon the urging of his father he studied law. But when the time came to appear for his final bar examination, terror so gripped him that he attempted suicide. He spent 18 months in an "insane asylum." A brief ray of hope pierced his soul when he read Rom. 3:25. This, in turn, led to serious study of the Bible which resulted in his conversion when he was 33.

His joy was enhanced when he met and became close friends with Pastor and Mrs. Morley Unwin. The death of Pastor Unwin three years later brought more sorrow. John Newton stepped in and invited Cowper to move to Olney where there was an opening for him to become pastor of a church. During the next 20 years the friendship between these two men deepened. Together they wrote hymns. Cowper published 67, translated Homer, published a highly praised volume of secular poems and a literary poem, "John Gilpin," a rollicking, humorous narrative.

Many renowned Christians have suffered from severe depression: Søren Kierkegaard, Charles Spurgeon, and J. B. Phillips, to name a few. All experienced unusual periods of creativity following each recovery. For instance, Phillips wrote up to three books a year.

We may not experience severe depression, but we can learn from these Christians not to become discouraged when we are depressed, but instead believe that afterwards creative acts can follow.

Gracious Creator God, help me understand in what form creative acts can follow my periods of depression also.

Day 2   Acts 9:10-19   "God moves in a mysterious way."

Wrong Number?

A weekend retreat had brought a young woman named Susan to the hometown of a friend. "Why don't I surprise her with a call?" Susan thought. But the phone book listed four people with the same name. Which was her friend's telephone number?

Susan dialed the first number. The woman who answered was not Susan's friend, but her agitated voice betrayed distress. Susan apologized for the mistake, then impulsively asked, "Are you all right?"

The woman at the other end of the line began to weep. "Do you believe in angels?" she asked. "I was attempting to end my life when the phone rang."

A lengthy conversation followed, and the despairing woman was able to hear and grab hold of words of hope as she learned about the Christ who knew her suffering and could help her.

That morning when Susan had committed the day to the Lord, little did she realize the mysterious way God would work. Sometimes God works in ways like that. We haven't even been conscious of the Holy Spirit's leading.

Other times the Holy Spirit gently whispers to us. Perhaps you've had the experience of being prompted by the Holy Spirit to write a letter, make a phone call or a home visit. As you have obeyed, you have been greeted with: "You don't know how much I needed your letter!" Or phone call. Or visit.

We never err when we obey the whisperings of the Holy Spirit. Why then, I wonder, do we so often hesitate to let God set our daily and hourly agendas and why are we so frustrated when his agendas upset ours?

Loving, faithful God, teach us to be more sensitive and responsive to the promptings of your Holy Spirit in order that you may be able to reach others through us.

Day 3   Rom. 8:28-39   "Behind a frowning providence."

What Hope Is There?

Saturday evening, August 19, 1944, 45-year-old Bishop Hans Lilje of Berlin answered the persistent ringing of his doorbell to find two Gestapo officials outside. Hours later Lilje heard the clank of a heavy iron door locking him in. The following months were filled with interrogations, hunger, and sleeplessness. Lilje's cell was lighted day and night and if he fell asleep, guards roughly awakened him. Outside, sirens whined and bombs exploded. On top of it all, anxiety over both his own future and his family's tormented him. Yet out of those months Lilje was able to trace the merciful face of God. How? By the enriched spiritual life God granted him.

The enrichment began with a journey into the "valley of the shadow," as he expressed it. The journey into the valley began when, as though a TV was flicked on, his past played itself out before him on a screen. "What a chain of dark memories is woven," he wrote, "when we look back at our life in the face of eternity" (*The Valley of the Shadow,* The Muhlenberg Press, 1950). He longed to turn off the "TV" but couldn't. His feeling of helplessness increased. His past was past. He could not alter it. He could only throw himself on the mercy of God. As he did new qualities of character blossomed and grew.

Over and over during his life King David experienced that his only hope was to throw himself on the mercy of God. Reviewing his past brought remorse to him too. Once, too late did he realize what not disciplining his son would lead to when Adonijah attempted a coup against his father. We read that David "had never interfered with [Adonijah] by asking, 'why do you behave as you do?' " (1 Kings 1:6).

Do you feel completely helpless to change your situation, your past, or the situation of a loved one? Though you wish you could step back in time and make some different choices and do things differently, you know you can't. What can you do? Cast yourself on the mercy of God. As you do, although your situation might not change, *you* can change as you slowly and patiently trace, by faith, God's compassionate, tender face.

I need your help to do this, dear Lord. Help me.

Day 4   Exod. 17:1-7   "Blind unbelief is sure to err."

Time to Take Responsibility

"Why did you bring us to this terrible place? Why couldn't we have stayed in Egypt?" the children of Israel asked Moses.

They had come to Rephidim expecting water, and there was none. It was the first month of the 40th year in the wilderness for this huge community of mournful movers. The new generation could not know how intolerable the situation in Egypt had been. The years probably had blotted out some of the harshest memories even for the old folks, as time has a way of doing. All of them forgot it was only their fathers' unbelief that had put them in this holding position in regard to entering Canaan. Thirty-eight years earlier Caleb and Joshua had tried to reassure them that God would take care of the giants the spies had reported having seen in Canaan. But jittery with fear, the people had rebelled against their leaders; rebellion had led to God's anger. That, in turn, had resulted in 40 years of wandering in the wilderness.

All this they now forgot. They blamed God instead of accepting responsibility for the consequences of their own sins.

Sometimes we do the same. We move or change jobs, hoping to earn more or have a better life. Things don't work out. Sometimes a child, following our example of drinking alcohol, for instance, is not able to control it. Or we neglect our kids while they are growing up, and then they neglect us when we're old. Or we nag and nag until our spouse walks out on us. And what do we do? We wail and cry, "Why, Lord, did you let this happen to us?"

Perhaps in more circumstances than we care to admit we need to learn to accept responsibility for our actions and confess to God what needs to be confessed. Then only will we be able to learn from our mistakes and sins.

Forgive us, righteous God, when we blame you for what has resulted because of our own sins. Give us a truly penitent spirit. Teach us to love and trust you more.

Day 5   Col. 3:12   "You fearful saints, fresh courage take."

Long-Lasting Effects

Do you ever get discouraged when a dream you've cherished never seems to be realized? William Tans'ur, the composer of the melody for this hymn, did. Many times. Permanent, profitable employment for a musician then, as now, was hard to find. Tans'ur wandered from town to town, teaching music and psalmody and serving as an organist. Finally he settled down selling books and teaching music. But he continued gathering materials for the book of psalm tunes and anthems he hoped to publish.

At last the day came. A publisher accepted his manuscript. His joy doubled when the publisher accepted yet another manuscript of his: *New Music Grammar.* The grammar was sold for over 80 years and outlived Tans'ur. And the melody of this hymn, known as Bangor, named for a city in Wales, has been sung by tens of thousands worldwide for the past 200 years. A town in Maine bears the name Bangor also, because the man registering the town was asked what the name of the town was to be. "Bangor!" he said impulsively, naming the tune he had been humming.

We do not know how short or long-lasting the effect of our lives will be. Nor do we know what effect our words or deeds are having on those whose lives we touch daily. But one thing is sure: we do not move through any day without influencing someone in one way or another. We either assist others to become what God wants them to be or we pull them down.

I wonder what effect Stephen's shining face and his prayer of forgiveness, uttered as the rocks were battering the life out of him, had on proud young Saul standing by, giving consent to his death? What did it do to Peter to have Jesus look at him in the courtyard just after the crowing of the cock, which like the tolling of a bell, had announced Peter's threefold denial?

Because people are creatures destined to live forever, how significant our influence on them becomes! Dare we do less than begin every day seeking our Lord's help so that we may be so in tune with God that people meeting us will meet Jesus?

Look through my eyes; speak through my lips, O Lord.

Day 6   Genesis 39   "The clouds . . . are big with mercy."

Storms Give New Life

Extremely hard, water-resistant shells coat the seeds of the Smoke tree, a "wash woodland" species that grows in the Southern California deserts. So resistant to water-penetration is the coat that even if you left the seed soaking in water for over a year, the seed would not sprout. The only hope for germination is to scrape and scratch the shell so water can permeate.

In the desert, cloudbursts undertake this task. Torrential rains sweep over the desert floor sending rocks and sand grinding against each other in the flood waters, ripping up and destroying vegetation. But, at the same time, the rocks and sands bruise the seeds of the Smoke tree, breaking the shells and allowing the water to penetrate. Germination follows, and soon little Smoke trees are sprouting to provide new covering for the desert floor. In this way the same flood waters that destroy also make it possible for new life to come.

Young Joseph's pride, left unschooled, easily could have hardened into an impenetrable core of lofty superiority. But "God was with Joseph," we read (Gen. 39:2-5). The grinding began when his brothers sold him to strangers who carried him to a far-off land. The battering continued when his master's wife falsely accused him of solicitation and Joseph was flung in prison. Still the wheels ground on when release was promised and then forgotten. But at last Joseph emerged. Such vibrant life had sprung from the penetrated hard core that he was able to rise to heights of power without it turning his head. When his brothers came seeking help (not knowing who he was), he was able to forgive them and provide a home for them in their need.

We may not be aware of our hard shells of resistance that need penetrating. Cracking open our shell always hurts, but if we allow the storms sweeping over us—threatening to destroy us, we think—to do their work, new life will burst forth in us that will bring blessing to others.

We shrink back from being bruised and battered, O God, but is it possible that sometimes it happens because we have a hard shell that needs to be cracked? Give us understanding.

Week 23

He Leadeth Me: Oh, Blessed Thought!

Joseph H. Gilmore, 1834–1918, alt. William B. Bradbury, 1816–1868

1 He leadeth me: oh, blessed thought! Oh, words with heav'nly comfort fraught!
2 Sometimes mid scenes of deepest gloom, Sometimes where Eden's bowers bloom,
3 Lord, I would clasp thy hand in mine, Nor ever murmur nor repine;
4 And when my task on earth is done, When by thy grace the vict'ry's won,

What-e'er I do, wher-e'er I be, Still 'tis God's hand that leadeth me.
By waters calm, o'er troubled sea, Still 'tis God's hand that leadeth me.
Content, whatever lot I see, Since 'tis my God that leadeth me.
E'en death's cold wave I will not flee, Since God through Jordan leadeth me.

Refrain

He leadeth me, he leadeth me, By his own hand he leadeth me.
His faithful foll'wer I would be, For by his hand he leadeth me.

Day 1   Psalm 23   "Still 'tis God's hand that leadeth me."

Knowing the One Leading

When Joseph Henry Gilmore, a Baptist preacher and professor of rhetoric, logic, and English literature at the University of Rochester, wrote this hymn in March 1862, he didn't plan to submit it for publication. He simply wrote it as part of a lecture on Psalm 23 he was preparing to give at a midweek service. But his wife thought it so good she sent it to the Boston *Watchman and Reflector* where it was published December 4, 1862.

Though we know the date Gilmore wrote the hymn, we do not know when David wrote the lovely psalm which inspired the hymn. Was David a shepherd boy tending his sheep? Or was he an old man, full of years and long of memory? Probably the latter. Why? Because after we have walked with the Lord many years we can trace, in retrospect, his leading in our lives. And having experienced his faithfulness over and over, it does become easier to sing, "Whate'er I do, wher'er I be, still 'tis God's hand that leadeth me."

The difference familiarity and trust makes was portrayed for us one day when we were driving in Turkey. We had to stop to allow a shepherd to lead his flock across the road to pastureland on the other side. As we watched we observed one sheep who kept darting away. Repeatedly the shepherd had to send his dog after him.

"Why doesn't that one sheep follow the shepherd like all the other sheep do?" I asked our driver.

He forwarded my question to the shepherd, speaking in the shepherd's mother tongue. The shepherd rattled off an answer as he took off running to retrieve the errant sheep once again.

"He says," our driver explained, "that he just bought this sheep yesterday, and it doesn't know his voice or trust him yet."

O loving God, help me welcome each time my faith is tested, knowing as I prove your faithfulness I will be able to trust you more and more.

Day 2 Isa. 42:5-9 "Lord, I would clasp thy hand in mine."

Hanging On Isn't Enough

Our little girl was learning to walk, but for some reason she would not let me hold her hands but insisted on hanging on to two of my fingers with each of her hands. Time after time her knees would sag, her grasp on my fingers would loosen, and down she would go.

"If you'd only let me hold your hands, I'd keep you on your feet when you stumble," I said to her, but of course babies that young can't understand adult talk (or else pretend not to), so the tumbles continued.

But Janet wasn't the only one who had to learn to let someone stronger hold on to her hand. Young Moses tried to obtain justice for his people in his own way and became so frightened at the results that he ran away. The disciples, flushed with early success, failed when confronted with a boy possessed by a spirit (Mark 9:17-29). Jesus had to stretch out his hand to Peter to grab hold of him as he was sinking in the sea. Let's face it. Left on our own, we're not as able or as strong as we'd like to think we are. Trying to meet in our own strength the demands life places on us is as futile as trying to fill the sails of a sailboat by blowing on them.

Jesus knows this. He knows that even those of us who are loudest in declaring our loyalty to him are capable of not only failing in an undertaking but capable even of falling away. The apostle Paul was painfully aware of this possibility too. "If you think you are standing firm, be careful that you don't fall!" he warned the Christians at Corinth (1 Cor. 10:12).

Then, lest the Christians focus on the possibility of failure and become immobilized for action, Paul hastened to reassure them that "God is faithful; he will not let you be tempted beyond what you can bear. But when you are tempted, he will also provide a way out so that you can stand up under it" (1 Cor. 10:13).

Allow God to hold your hand and lead you. In response, you can put your hands in his, joyfully, trustingly.

Oh, take my hand, dear Lord, and lead me all the way home.

Day 3   2 Cor. 11:22–12:10   "Nor ever murmur nor repine."

Can We Not Complain?

In a talk given in Tokyo in September 1984, Bishop K. H. Ting said the instruction given to the Laodicean church recorded in Revelation became the experience of the Chinese Christians during the years from 1966–1976 when the Chinese church was experiencing trial.

They could trace the hand of God in the sufferings that came to them, and so they were able to endure, Bishop Ting recounted.

"I do not think we were terribly sad those days, because many colleagues were suffering," Ting said. "In fact, if one of us was spared, we would feel rather badly about it, as if he or she had deserted the suffering brothers and sisters." Suffering, they felt, like joy, was meant to be shared.

It was the joy of the resurrection, the joy of knowing the risen Christ that carried them during those years, Ting continued. The Easter message, he declared, was "the most important and precious message God has given us in the last 35 years. The resurrection truth tells us it is through loss, poverty, suffering, and death that life is sustained. Life depends on the risen Christ. That a person who has died should come to life again is to all common sense an absurd claim. Yet almost one-fourth of all humankind is committed to the resurrection story of Jesus Christ."

Bishop Ting was asked how this could be.

"It is because this message of hope has touched the chord of hope in the ears of so many who simply refuse to accept defeat, humiliation, suffering, darkness, and death as ultimate," Ting said. "In the midst of all vicissitudes they have learned to look to the risen Christ."

Sooner or later similar opportunities are offered us. To talk and write about accepting whatever comes to us without murmuring is easy. To do so is something else. But if we can fix our eyes steadfastly on the risen Christ and the resurrection hope he offers us, it can become a reality for us too.

O, our risen Christ, may your living presence with us become more real to us every day.

Day 4   Deut. 32:9-12   "His faithful foll'wer I would be."

When God Calls

As children we sometimes would blindfold one another and then take turns leading the blindfolded one through a labyrinth of chairs we had set up, and up and down a plank balanced on something solid. Usually our play was noisy with laughter, giggles, and glee. Years later in an adult group I saw the same exercise conducted to see what degree of trust we had in the person leading us when we couldn't see. That adult group was much quieter. The ones being led shuffled along slowly and carefully, their one free arm outstretched to identify obstacles. Watching us, I concluded that we adults have much more difficulty following when we can't see where we're being led than children do.

However, it would seem that God almost delights in calling us to follow him in blindfolded ventures even though we aren't too eager to play with him. He called Moses to lead the children of Israel from Egypt into the wilderness. All they had to go on was a promise that he would bring them to a land they could call their own. He called Joshua to fill the size 13 shoes of his predecessor Moses, Nehemiah to rebuild the walls of Jerusalem, Jeremiah to become an unpopular prophet, Amos to leave the quiet of his sheepfold to proclaim judgment to a proud, stubborn people, and Hosea to marry a harlot.

Those called were really scared. "Woe to me! I am ruined!" was Isaiah's first response when God confronted him. When the Lord talked to Moses about going to Pharaoh, Moses asked, "Who am I that I should go?" Joshua must have been scared because three times the Lord said to him, "Be strong and courageous."

Is God calling you to venture out on some new undertaking for which you are not sure you are able? Remember: when he calls, he empowers. "You will receive power when the Holy Spirit comes on you" (Acts 1:8). That promise is for you. "Surely I will be with you always." That's for you too. And as with a sheep and the shepherd, we need not know where the path is leading us as long as we know the one we're following.

Forgive me for so often being a coward, Lord.

Day 5   Ps. 16:5-11   "Sometimes where Eden's bowers bloom."

Use Sunny Days Wisely

The forest ranger standing beside us outlined the rings on the sawed trunk of the giant tree lying on the ground.

"The size of the rings indicates the growth of the tree each year," he explained. "When moisture and sun were rightly balanced, and when no insects or disease plagued the tree, it grew most." He indicated some rings that were broader than others.

But not only trees grow best when conditions are favorable. Nations do too. One of the reasons for the slowed growth of some African countries has been the disruptive effect of numerous civil wars. A nation at peace prospers.

Generally speaking, Christ's kingdom grows best when circumstances are fortuitous. This surely was true in many respects when the Christian church was founded. At that time the world was more at peace under the Roman rule than it had been for decades. The Romans had built well-engineered, paved roads, and travel over them was comparatively safe. The business and educated world spoke a common language—Greek. The Jewish business people, who had emigrated far and wide, had introduced monotheism to the peoples among whom they lived. All of this contributed to the rapid growth of the church later.

But not only trees and nations and churches thrive best when "Eden's bowers bloom," but individuals do too. When is the best time to build up spiritual resources? When life flows smoothly. Years when we are brim full of good health. It is very difficult—almost impossible—to develop faith in times of severe testing. Usually a crisis merely reveals what was already there. Sunny times will come also after sorrow's sharp edge has been dulled, offering us the opportunity to reflect on and draw profit from the past. Samuel Rutherford noted: "No cross should be old to us. We should not cast away our crosses as we do old clothes. We may make an old cross new in use and as fruitful as in its beginning."

So when God leads you where "Eden's bowers bloom," rejoice.

Help me discipline myself, O Lord, in developing my faith so when the winds of trouble blow I'll be able to bend, not break.

Day 6   2 Cor. 5:1-15   "E'en death's cold wave I will not flee."

Death Conquered through Death

It was cleaning day, and Thai, our pet Siamese cat, followed me from room to room, meowing most pitifully. She was so weak she could keep her balance only by spreading her legs as she walked. From time to time I would stop and pick her up and hold her; and if you could say a cat sobs, Thai sobbed. As the hours passed, her cries became louder and more frequent, and I knew that Thai indeed was dying. The telephone ringing called me away. When I came back, the plaintive meowing had stopped. Thai was dead.

If death is so distressing for animals who die, but who are not under the wrath of God, how much more should humans who die under the wrath of God cry out, Luther said. Animals simply die, he stated. Humans die to await the resurrection and the judgment.

Luther further differentiated between the death of animals and humans. As he stated, death is something that has intruded, something that has entered us humans from outside. God did not intend originally that we should die, so death for us is unnatural. When God made us in his image, that image included the provision that we should not know death but like God be possessors of eternal life. But through sin that image was lost, and God's wrath descended and rested on us. Eternal life became eternal death, a death we cannot escape or lift from ourselves. Only God can lift it from us, but thank God, he can and has and does and will (*What Luther Says*, Concordia, 1959).

Thus we see that in the New Testament, judgment and death are placed in the background. This is not to say death is denied. It isn't. Golgotha remains grim, bloody, and terrible. The marks of death remain on the palms of the risen Christ. But Christ has overcome death by his own death and resurrection. As Luther expressed it, death—to believers—is already dead and can hide nothing terrible behind its grinning mask. Thus with Paul we can cry, "Where, O death, is your victory? Where, O death, is your sting?" (1 Cor. 15:55).

Thank you, God, for the victory over death that is ours in our Lord Jesus Christ.

Day 1   Mark 6:30-46   "We blossom and flourish."

Is There Really No Time?

What do you do to refresh yourself when weary? Listen to music? Watch TV? Read? Pray? Swim, bicycle, walk, or jog? Shop? Cook? Eat? Sleep? W. Chalmers Smith, the author of this hymn, wrote poetry, as he expressed it, "as a retreat from the burden of my labors." For 44 years he served as pastor, bishop, and finally moderator of the Assembly of the Free Church in Scotland. Writing poetry, Smith said, allowed him to give expression to some of the thoughts and feelings of his heart which he could not express from the pulpit. Writing poetry refreshed and energized him.

As we meditate on the majestic words of this hymn, so rich in meaning, we can understand how writing it renewed Smith. For the hymn takes our eyes off ourselves, our crazy world, and our problems. Instead it guides us in looking to the invisible, sovereign God whose ways and intentions are sometimes hidden from us, but who continues as the God in motion, always working toward the completion of his purposes.

Even Jesus, while on earth, found it necessary to discipline himself to withdraw, from time to time, to a place where he could stay for a period with his God, to commune with him, listen to him, and be instructed by him. If Jesus found this absolutely necessary, how much more should we.

Some of our time should be spent alone with God, dwelling in the Word, for through the Word God speaks to us. We respond in prayer, praise, in quietly sitting in worship before him, or in offering ourselves up again to him.

If we do not take time for this, we shall soon be found drained and empty. Do we find it difficult to maintain regularity and constancy in our personal devotional life? Do we excuse ourselves, saying we've been too busy; there's been no time? Perhaps we need to ask ourselves, as Carlo Caretto asked in *The God Who Comes,* "Have you not been praying, not seeking him personally because you have no time or because you don't love him?"

Loving Savior, enable me to love you more and to value more greatly the fountain of refreshment that comes from communing with you that you have made available for me.

Day 2   John 1:18   "Invisible."

The Invisible God

During the early era of Israel's history, references are made to people "seeing" God, but when described, what they saw were flames or a brilliant, almost blinding light (Exod. 24:9-11; Hab. 3:3,4) or the indistinct outlines of a human form (Ezek. 1:25-28; Dan. 7:9 and 10:9). Then in the account of Moses and the burning bush all outlines fade and only a whispered voice is left, the voice of someone very close.

But in spite of God remaining the invisible, hidden God, Israel experienced God's presence with them. For a while the ark and the cloud were visible expressions of God's presence, but then these too disappeared.

Next came the New Testament era when Christ, who is of one essence and substance with the Father and yet distinct from the Father, took on human form, being born as a baby. The Word became visible and touchable. As John stated in his letter, he would write only about that which he had seen with his eyes and had looked at (1 John 1:1-4). Jesus, by taking on human form, became, as one little girl in Sunday School explained, "the best picture God ever had taken of himself."

But now for us Jesus too has become invisible. We have his promise that one day we shall see him as he is, but we cannot claim that promise yet. But though we cannot see him, he speaks to us through his Word and through the soft whisperings of his Spirit. We know his presence with us in Baptism and at his table. We also experience his coming to us in the persons of our brothers and sisters in Christ who stand by our sides in times of need. We recognize him too in the poor and needy and also in the ways in which he orders our lives.

And so we do not complain because our God is invisible. His invisibility adds to his mystery, and if mystery did not enshroud him, would he still be God? Would we really want a God whom we could see? I think not. Instead, in reverence and awe we worship and adore our invisible yet ever-present, loving God.

Grant, O God, that each day I may give some time to strengthen my hold on the unseen world.

Day 3   Psalm 13   "Hid from our eyes."

The Hiddenness of God

Our God, in some respects, remains for us a hidden God. Sometimes, however, he reveals a little of that mysterious aspect of his being. When he does, we may react differently. Moses trembled when the bush burned and God warned him not to come closer. Abraham mutely obeyed the command he couldn't understand to sacrifice his only son. Job reeled, was stunned, and then angered by the torrent of tragedies that leveled him. Jesus, who is described as being so close to God that he lay in the bosom of the Father, asked God why he had abandoned him. All of these cried out, in one way or another, "God, where are you in all this? What are you doing? Who are you, you terrible God?"

We too know these times. When these times come, if we do not affirm our faith in God even though we cannot understand what he is doing or allowing to happen, we shall find terror and repulsion towards God rising in our hearts. But if we affirm that God, though hidden, is in control, then trust, self-dedication, love, and even praise will replace the terror. And peace will follow.

But to be able to make this affirmation of faith, we must have become convinced through previous experiences that God is loving and trustworthy. The Israelites learned this as they obeyed God's law which was clearly stated and saw how obeying it was actually *good.* Then they were able to continue to trust him when the clouds enclosed him, the fire kept them at a distance, and the demands God made seemed unreasonable. But when they disobeyed God's law, terror seized their hearts when God drew near.

What emotions grip us when the presence of God becomes real to us? Love or anxiety? Do we want to draw closer or do we pull back in fear? Perhaps we shall never get beyond feeling some anxiety as we think of standing before a holy God, especially if we are conscious as death draws near. But if love and trust have characterized our relationship with God, that anxiety perhaps can more accurately be called awe.

O God, even though I can't see you, let me keep your commands.

Day 4   Ezekiel 1   "Unresting, unhasting."

God Is On the Move

In describing God as "unresting, unhasting," the hymn writer sees God moving and acting in a harmonious rhythm. His action is first described in creation. "The Spirit of God *was hovering* over the waters," we read in Genesis 1:2.

God continues infusing life in all his creation. Job acknowledged that the "breath of the Almighty *gives me life*" (Job 33:4—italics added). Dorothy Faber, a victim of systemic lupus, wrote: "Without [Christ] there would have been no hope, no reason to engage in the daily bout with a disease that eats you up a little at a time. Without Him I could never have fooled the medical experts all these years."

God is also at work renewing the face of the earth (Ps. 104:30). Each part of the rhythm of life—night following day, spring, summer, autumn following summer, then winter—makes its own contribution in restoring and replenishing the earth.

God continues at work in our lives. From time to time he stirs up our nests, gently pushing us out, coaxing and urging us to do that which we have not done before. He hovers over us, ready to catch us if we fall (Deut. 32:11), and to shield and protect us from all who would harm us (Isa. 31:5).

Nor is God indifferent to the pain, distress, and sorrow of the oppressed. Even in situations that appear hopeless, he is at work. He also seeks out those who it seems have been dead for a long, long time and resuscitates them (Ezek. 37).

And, finally, God is the Sovereign God of history, bringing history to completion. The time will come when he will say, "I am making everything new," and then, "It is done." (Rev. 21:5-6).

And so we know him as the God active in creation, as the Creator renewing the earth, the Mediator pleading the cause of the oppressed, the Reviver of the dead, and the Sovereign God in control of history. But we also know him as the loving God at work in our lives, even during dry seasons when we perceive no growth or when we may even feel we are regressing.

O Father, I pray for faith to see your purpose of love unfolding in the circumstances and happenings of my life.

Day 5   Mic. 6:8   "Thy justice . . . goodness and love."

Linking Justice and Love

When a corporation was purchased by a larger corporation, its top executive was abruptly dropped from first floor to fourth. The news shocked his friends. During his 25 years of leadership and hard work, the company had enjoyed economic growth and stability. "Why then was he passed by?" they asked.

In reply, the former director explained he was only three years from retirement. The one chosen to become the chief executive of the new company was young, brilliant, energetic, creative, and aggressive. "The choice makes sense," he said. "However, during these weeks of reorganization many of us who have worked hard and been loyal to our company have been treated by the top management like horses—even worse than horses—in an almost inhuman and cruel way. This denies the principle that fairness should always be accompanied by goodness and love."

In his hymn Smith links the three together: God's justice, his goodness, and his love. Luther also emphasized the necessity of coupling justice with love. Fairness even in legal judgments, Luther stated, can spring only from an alliance of justice and love, not from one or the other alone. So too the decision by the governing board to pass over the former director in preference to a younger one may have been considered fair for the sake of the new organization. But to link justice with goodness and love, careful consideration should have been given to the fact that the decision, and more especially the way in which it was implemented, involved human lives and souls and their happiness.

When times come for us to administer justice—even if it be only in disciplining our children—let us always remember to "let the apple lie alongside the rod," as Luther admonished. And if we are faced with making a decision that may seem better for the common good though painful for the individual, as sometimes happens in families, congregations, or companies, let us be sure that compassion, mercy, and goodness characterize the way we expedite the decision.

Just God, keep me honorable and just in all my dealings.

Day 6 John 1:1-13   "To all, life thou givest."

Creative Observers

Paul, speaking to the Greeks in Athens, reminded them that "[the God who made the world] himself gives all men life and breath and everything else. . . . 'For in him we live and move and have our being.' " Then Paul concluded, "As some of your own poets have said, 'We are his offspring' " (Acts 17:24-28).

So then, natural life is a gift from God, given when "the Lord God formed the man from the dust of the ground and breathed into his nostrils *the breath of life, and man became a living being*" (Gen. 2:7—italics added). Life, natural life, is sacred.

That life, however, was marred by sin, so unless it is quickened into a new life or infused with a new spiritual quality, it will not continue after death as the God-honoring life God meant it to be. Because of that we could even say that people who have not yet received a new spiritual life from God are like dead people walking around.

But the good news is that because they have been given natural life by God, they carry in them the seeds or the possibilities of blossoming into life with Christ. As the hymn writer wrote: "to all, life thou givest," and "in all life thou livest."

Anne Lindbergh, the American writer, in a tribute to a friend of hers who had died, referred to him as one who could see people creatively—not only as they are, but as they are meant to be. She called her friend a creative observer.

We too can become creative observers for those in whom Christ has not yet been formed. As we pray for them we can visualize Christ being formed in them with all the changes that will bring. In our interaction with them we can treat them as we would treat Christ—with love, courtesy, respect, and service, trusting the Holy Spirit to breathe into them the new life of the Spirit.

Father, I leave in your hands the coming of your spiritual life into the hearts of those for whom I pray, believing that my love is but a feeble shadow of yours.

Week 25

Take My Life, that I May Be

Frances R. Havergal, 1836–1879, alt.
William H. Havergal, 1793–1870

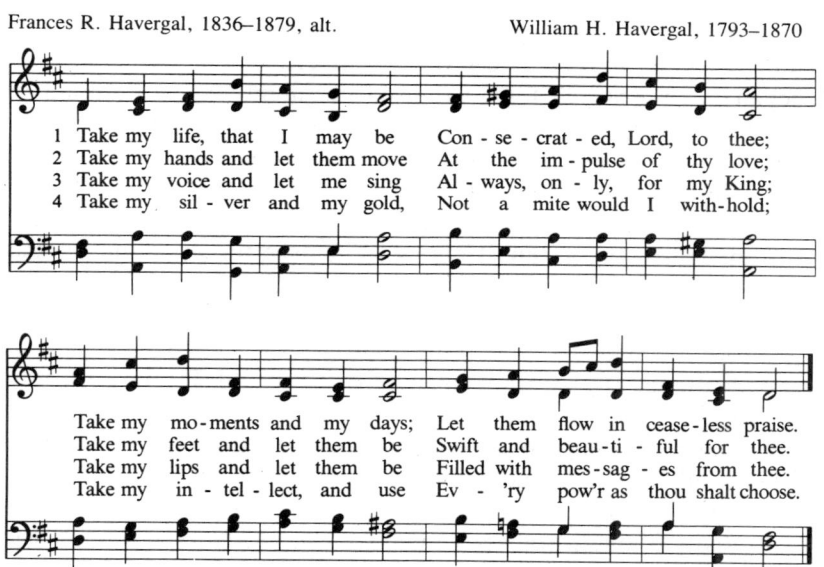

1. Take my life, that I may be
Con-se-crat-ed, Lord, to thee;
Take my mo-ments and my days;
Let them flow in cease-less praise.

2. Take my hands and let them move
At the im-pulse of thy love;
Take my feet and let them be
Swift and beau-ti-ful for thee.

3. Take my voice and let me sing
Al-ways, on-ly, for my King;
Take my lips and let them be
Filled with mes-sag-es from thee.

4. Take my sil-ver and my gold,
Not a mite would I with-hold;
Take my in-tel-lect, and use
Ev-'ry pow'r as thou shalt choose.

5. Take my will and make it thine;
It shall be no longer mine.
Take my heart, it is thine own;
It shall be thy royal throne.

6. Take my love; my Lord, I pour
At thy feet its treasure store;
Take myself, and I will be
Ever, only, all for thee.

Day 1   Rom. 12:1-8   "Take my life."

Seek First the Kingdom

William H. Havergal, rector and musician, fondly called his little daughter, Frances, "Little Quicksilver." Almost as soon as she began to read at age four, she used her highly retentive mind to memorize Scripture. By the end of her life she had tucked away in her memory the Psalms, Isaiah, the minor prophets, and the entire New Testament except Acts. When her able mind directed its attention to languages, Frances became fluent in French, German, Italian, Latin, Greek, and Hebrew. When she turned to music, she soon was able to play the classical pieces of the masters from memory. But study of the Bible received most of her attention. Since her love of God was the motivating center of her life, she wanted to keep learning. During summer months she would sit down to study at 7:00 A.M., in the winter, at 8:00. Teaching Sunday school and speaking at meetings occupied much of her time. Once, so tired from it all, she exclaimed that she hoped when she got to heaven "the angels will have orders to let me alone a bit."

Varied though Frances's interests and exceptional though her talents, she always kept her feet solidly planted in seeking first the kingdom of God. The background to this week's hymn portrays this. Frances had gone to visit friends for five days. "There were ten in the house," she wrote, "some were unconverted but long prayed for, some converted but not rejoicing Christians. God gave me the prayer, 'Lord, give me all in this house.' And he just did. Before I left the house, everyone had got a blessing. The last night I was too happy to sleep and passed most of the night in renewal of my consecration, and these little couplets formed themselves and chimed in my heart till they finished with 'ever only, all for Thee!' " (*101 Hymn Stories,* 1982).

When did we last experience the joy of seeing people come to faith in Christ? If it has been a long time, what may be some of the reasons? What difference would it make in our lives if we saw it happening?

Enable me to be an effective witness for you, O Savior.

Day 2   Col. 3:17   "Take my hands."

Trottin' Around the House with Joy

If it ever occurred to Esther Edwards Burr that spending her time raising two small children and cooking and caring for a never-ending stream of guests was not serving Christ, she didn't hint at it in her letters to her closest friend, Sarah Prince. When she was only 18, Esther, the daughter of Jonathan and Sarah Edwards, had married 38-year-old Rev. Aaron Burr, the superintendent of the College of New Jersey, which later became Princeton University.

Excerpts from her letters give insight into Esther's life. "Company come and go—come and go—continually it is Rap, Rap—is the President at home all day. . . . All the time I have with Mr. Burr (her husband) is at the Table; Mr. Tennet and he begrudge one minnit from College. . . . This is the first vacant moment I have had since Saturday last—yes, every moment has been taken up with company or some necessary duty. . . . For a month past hant done a shillings worth of Work, but 'tis Trot, Trot around the house, day after day. . . . I am weaning Aaron and he makes a great Noise about it" (*The Journal Entries of Esther Edwards Burr,* Yale University Press, 1984).

But these remarks tell only one side of the story. In almost every letter she expresses love for God and praise for his goodness. "When I look back on the year past and take a view of the Numberless Mercies I have been the subject of, I stand amazed at God's goodness to such an Ill-deserving, Hell-deserving Creature [as] I am." Her joy at the awakening taking place at the College reverberates throughout her letters. "Mr. Burr . . . comes home greatly affected and we sit and talk till late." She writes of her desire to spend more time in prayer and meditation but doesn't tell if she ever found it possible. As we continue to read her letters, we note that though she was often frustrated, she realized that her own feelings and preferences were poor guides. Instead she understood that spiritual life does not consist in mere individual betterment but in a free, unconditional response to the Spirit's call to serve Christ in whatever circumstances we find ourselves. Understanding this can relieve frustration and enables us also to keep "trottin'."

Dear Lord, I don't think I'll ever do great things, but help me do in a great way the little things life has assigned me.

Day 3   Rom. 8:28   "Take my intellect, and use."

When Limitations Release Us

Frances Havergal's artistry both as a concert pianist and soloist meant that concert halls were vying with each other to book her as a performing artist. In between her performances, Frances reveled in the physical strength and vitality of her body as she climbed peak after peak in the Swiss Alps. But then periods of illness started to harass her and drain away her strength. As she became weaker and weaker, Frances began to reevaluate her priorities. As a result she determined to present only concerts of sacred music. As strength declined farther, she concentrated on doing what she could: writing letters and poetry.

During her life span of only 43 years, Frances was incapacitated by illness 21 years. She used that time developing her skill as a poet, seeking to interpret her spiritual experiences in verse. She did not consider her poetry to be of high quality but said simply she had given her talent, such as it was, to God, to be used as he could. "For me," she said, "writing is praying." By the end of her life she had filled six volumes with her poetry. Many poems were set to music and continue to be sung as dearly loved hymns. Her father wrote the music for this hymn.

We may ask if we would have Frances Havergal's rich legacy of hymns today if the restrictions illness imposed had not forced her to concentrate on developing her art as a poet. Restricted lives can become very effective. People unhampered by serious limitations sometimes find it difficult to sift out their most promising strengths and develop them fully. Instead, all too often energies are dissipated over a wide array of activities. As a result many of us do not become really proficient or excel in any. Periodically we need to pause and ask ourselves if we are involved in so many things that we are not significantly effective in any. Focused lives frequently are the most potent.

Lord, the pressure is on us to be as busy as ants. Help us to learn to be quiet and to listen for your voice of direction.

Day 4   2 Cor. 8:1-7   "Not a mite would I withhold."

Has Your Wallet Been Baptized?

Years ago when whole armies of the Franks were baptized by immersion, many of the warriors held their swords high so they wouldn't get wet. Then they could say, "These were not baptized," and they then felt free to do as they pleased with their right hand and their sword.

Paul Tillich noted, "Real religion is first of all an open hand to receive gifts from the Lord and Giver of all; and secondly, it is a helping hand to distribute gifts to any and all who are in need. . . . It is a two-handed religion that we live."

Frances Havergal lived a two-handed religion. Two years after she composed this hymn, she wrote to a friend, "The Lord has shown me another little step, and, of course, I have taken it with extreme delight. 'Take my silver and my gold,' now means shipping off all my ornaments to the Church Missionary House, including a jewel cabinet that is fit for a countess, where all will be accepted and disposed of for me. I retain only a brooch for daily wearing and a locket. Nearly fifty articles are being packed. I don't think I ever packed a box with such pleasure" (*101 Hymn Stories,* Kregel, 1982).

For the Philippian Christians, putting their means at God's disposal meant, among other things, sending money to Paul during his time of house imprisonment (Phil. 4:14-16). For the Christians in Macedonia and Achaia, it meant making a contribution for the needs of the poor in Jerusalem (Rom. 15:26). For James, Jesus' brother, it meant doing what he could to prevent poverty. Maimonides, one of the Jewish rabbinical teachers, declared that giving to prevent poverty is the most desirable form of giving. That is, we give so needy persons may be able to earn an honest living and not be forced in embarrassment to hold out a hand for charity. Church institutions that work with the poor provide a channel for us to give in this way.

Frances Havergal, along with the early Christians, found joy in giving extravagantly. To what extent do we know this joy?

We're often so afraid to give, God, of ourselves and that which we call our own. Forgive us. Set us free from fear.

Day 5 James 2:14-17 "Take my silver and my gold."

Cautious Christians

"I feel so good every time I say no," a woman said as she emerged from a department store with a parcel in her hand, containing only the one item she had gone in to buy. Living on a limited budget, she knew she could not afford to succumb to impulse buying. Yet immediately upon entering the store, the cheery yellow *Sale!* signs had coaxed and tempted her and the *One Day Only!* bright red signs had warned her that she had better buy immediately or miss getting in on bargains. Her resolution, made before she had entered the store, had helped her say no as she hurried past the signs and out the door with only the one item in her hand.

This is not to say we cannot linger at the sales racks and tables at times. Sometimes we are good stewards to do so. What, then, determines the difference? Certainly how much money we have. But even if we have the cash, our actual needs must be balanced against the needs of the rest of the family. Parents usually don't keep adding to their racks of clothing while their children go in tatters. Yet all too often, as Christians, we do not remember the needy in our worldwide family. Or we prefer not to think about them. Or we simply refuse to accept responsibility to care for them. As Reinhold Niebuhr once wrote in *Leaves from the Notebook of a Tamed Cynic:* "There is a discouraging pettiness about human nature which makes me hate myself each time I make an analysis of my inner motives and springs of action. . . . I make my own compromises all the time. . . . I am too cautious to be a Christian."

Yes, we find it easy and comfortable to offer all sorts of reasonable excuses and arguments as to why we cannot follow Christ's commands just as they stand. So we make our own adjustments, our own compromises. According to Niebuhr, most of us adjust our moral goals somewhere between the "reasonable ethic of moderation Aristotle taught and Christ's ethic of love. I hope," he added, "there is more of Christ than of Aristotle in my position. But I would not be too sure of it."

Search me, O God, and know my heart.

Day 6   Matt. 3:13-17; Luke 9:28-36; 22:39-46   "Take my will."

Fresh Commitment

Even as a child Frances Havergal felt the tug and pull of two natures struggling for control. "As for trying to be good," she wrote later, "that seemed to be of next to no use. It was like struggling in a quicksand, and the more you struggle, the more you sink" (*Lyric Religion,* Fleming H. Revell, 1981). Christ became real to her when she was 14, and with joy she committed herself to him. When she was 18, on her confirmation day, she made a fresh commitment to him. As her pastor laid his hands on her head, she felt herself alone in God's presence. "Defend, O Lord, this thy child with thy heavenly grace," her pastor prayed, "that she may continue thine forever." Thine forever! As Frances prayed that prayer joy filled her spirit to overflowing.

However, both of these experiences marked but the first of a series of dedications of herself to God. Again and again, as her situation changed, we read of her fresh commitments to Jesus.

An ongoing commitment to the Father's will was necessary for Jesus too, as, little by little, he began to understand what ultimately it would mean. It will be for us also. It is as though we are on an around-the-world trip. Each country we visit offers different experiences. After visiting some countries we aren't sure we want to go on. We think we'd rather turn around and go home. But our companion urges us to keep going, and so we take courage and do so.

Thus also we shall discover that following Jesus calls for an ever deeper investment of ourselves and a more conclusive saying yes to risk taking. If when we first started to follow Christ we saw all that was going to be involved, most of us would be scared off. So, tenderly and with understanding—because he has walked the way before us—Jesus leads us step by step, never asking more than we can, with his enabling, give. With love he entreats us to follow, for he knows that only then we find pure joy.

Lord Jesus, I thank you that I can trust you to lead me and provide for me and protect me.

Week 26

Now Thank We All Our God

Martin Rinkhart, 1586–1649
tr. Catherine Winkworth, 1829–1878

Johann Crüger, 1598–1662

1. Now thank we all our God With hearts and hands and voices, Who won-drous things has done, In whom his world rejoices; Who, from our mothers' arms, Has blest us on our way, With countless gifts of love, And still is ours to-day.

2. Oh, may this bounteous God Through all our life be near us, With ever joyful hearts And blessed peace to cheer us, And keep us in his grace, And guide us when perplexed, And free us from all harm In this world and the next.

3. All praise and thanks to God The Father now be given, The Son, and him who reigns With them in highest heaven, The one eternal God, Whom earth and heav'n adore; For thus it was, is now, And shall be evermore.

Day 1   Col. 3:7   "With heart and hands and voices."

Endurance

The war dragged on wearily, endlessly it seemed, a power struggle between Protestantism and Catholicism with political as well as religious implications and with land boundaries at stake. Martin Rinkhart, a 31-year-old Lutheran pastor, had just arrived at the pastorate in Eilenberg, Germany, his home town, when the war began. Son of a poor coppersmith, he had worked his way through the University of Leipzig.

Eilenberg was a walled city, and as the armies surged back and forth, peoples fleeing their homes sought refuge there, overcrowding the city. Famine and disease added to the suffering. In 1637 a plague swept through the city. When the other two pastors in the city died, Rinkhart was left alone to care for the suffering. There were 40 to 50 funerals to conduct daily. His wife died. He became ill but recovered. Wherever he went people stopped him, begging for food. He gave all he had and then mortgaged his future salary to give more. Three times armies invaded the city, causing more suffering. When the Swedish army came, the general demanded 30,000 thaler from the people. Rinkhart went to him. "We don't have the money," he said. "Can't you see we can barely stay alive?" "Armies need money," the general said coldly. Rinkhart turned to those who had come with him. "Children," he said. "We can find no mercy with men. Let us take refuge in God." And kneeling, he began to pray, and closed by singing Paul Eber's hymn, "When in the hour of utmost need." "All right, all right," the general said gruffly when Rinkhart got up, "we'll settle for 1,350 thaler."

For 30 years the war brutalized people, dragging into its nets eight nations, bringing great suffering to innocent civilians. Through all those dark years, with heart and hands and voice Rinkhart offered up a sacrifice of thanksgiving—writing and singing this hymn and others, and persistent in his care for the suffering. Thirty years! What a long, long time!

How small is my endurance, O God! Is it because I live so distantly from you? Forgive me. Unite my heart to yours.

Day 2   Ps. 105:1-5   "Who wondrous things has done."

Thankfulness

One day in November is never enough for me to express my thanksgiving. I need all year. I believe thanksgiving, to be authentic, needs to be "thanksliving." In the 1700s Cotton Mather pointed this out. It is pointless just to "*be* thankful," he said. "If we are really thankful, we will *do* something." So whenever Mather wanted to express gratitude, he did some specific act of good.

God has blessed most of us with friends and family. We can show our gratitude by trying to understand what is important to each one, and then do something for them that will be in tune with this. So, please God, help us to observe and listen.

God has blessed us with a church that nourishes and cares for us. We can respond by showing our thanks as we care for those who are hurting and as we thank those who make our church home the wonderful place it is.

God has placed us in a country unexcelled for all it offers us. As a token of thanks we can work to help bridge the gap that separates races, to insure liberty and justice for all, and to see that all are fed.

God gives health to our bodies. In thanks we can respond by caring for them better. We can also give of our means to bring medical care to those who do not have it.

God has given us the joyous opportunity to keep learning and growing. In gratitude we seek to use wisely the gifts he has given us, and also support those who are offering opportunities to others to learn and grow.

Most meaningful of all, God has revealed himself to us and brought faith in Jesus to birth in our hearts. In innumerable ways we have experienced his faithfulness and love. In thanksgiving we bear witness to his love whenever and by whatever means we can.

"O Lord my God, I will give you thanks forever," the psalmist wrote (Ps. 30:12). For what are you most deeply thankful and how can you best express your gratitude? Talk to the Lord about this.

Day 3   Ps. 65:11-13   "In whom his world rejoices."

All Nature Rejoices

Both the hymn writer and the psalmist saw God's earth rejoicing in his goodness. "You care for the land and water it" the psalmist wrote. "You crown the year with your bounty. . . . The grasslands of the desert overflow; the hills are clothed with gladness. The meadows are covered with flocks and the valleys are mantled with grain," and, as a result, "they shout for joy and sing" (Ps. 65:9, 11-13).

"Let the heavens rejoice, let the earth be glad . . . ," the psalmist writes in another place, "let the fields be jubilant, and everything in them. Then all the trees of the forest will sing for joy; they will sing before the Lord" (Ps. 96:11-13).

We, of course, can mar this concert by abusing the gifts given us to use carefully, by demanding that the earth produce too much, by leveling forests without thought, by polluting life-giving waters, by silencing birds.

We also see brokenness in nature even as we see it in ourselves. Storms, cyclones, earthquakes, and tidal waves from time to time shatter the song of praise. But the majority of time the earth is rejoicing.

We can learn to let earth and its produce assist us in our offerings of praise. I met a widow in the garden shop one day. "Tomorrow it'll be four years since Herbert died," she said. "I plant a rose bush at church every anniversary. It's my way of thanking God for the 42 wonderful years he gave us together."

My mother cherished trees. Every time the family moved she planted trees. "For those who come after me," she said. So it was when she gave my husband cash gifts at Christmas, he bought and planted fruit trees that continue to bear. It was our way of having nature help us say thanks to Mother for the values she taught us.

Maybe it would help us get in touch with nature better if we could think of ways that the earth and its produce could assist us in our thanksgiving to God.

Help me every day as I step outside to be conscious of how nature is praising you, O God, and may I not in any way hinder that praise from being offered.

Day 4   Prov. 22:6   *"Who from our mother's arms."*

The Fortunate Children

If we are parents, and if our children are going to be able to say they have been blessed by us on their way, to what should we give attention as we raise them?

Love your children. The greatest gift parents can give is love. Children need to know they are wanted and accepted just as they are. In most cases, the closest human counterpart to God's unconditional love is parental love. Show your children in many ways that you love them.

Define value and character goals for your children, and be sure these are in harmony with God's Word. As you pray for your children, hold before you a mental picture of the qualities you would like them to have.

Watch so that your life portrays Christ to them.

Invest time and interest in your children. "I wish Dad would play ball with me once in a while, and I wish Mom wouldn't have to work so hard that she's always tired," a young boy said.

Keep in touch with your children's teachers. Listen to what they say; don't be self-defensive and don't merely excuse your child if there is cause for concern.

Know your children's friends. Keep your home open to them. Choose your place of residence and your church home so good friends will be available.

Watch your speaking and listening. When does a parent say something too often—to teenagers especially? When he or she says it twice. Also listen to your children. Listening also includes being aware of feelings, actions, and subtle cues.

Have some realistic restrictions; if these are broken, deal with the disobedience promptly. Follow with words of grace and forgiveness.

Give praise, affirmation, and affection generously. In fact, we may sum up all of this in the words of the director of a home for troubled children: "Care for your children, just care for them and about them, and the rest will fall naturally in place."

O Heavenly Father, make me a better parent.

Day 5   Prov. 13:22a   "With countless gifts of love."

Gifts of Love

Mother loved to sing as she worked. I guess her singing was a natural expression of her attitude toward life. "Well, it surely isn't worth complaining about!" How often we had heard her say this! Mother's cheerful attitude towards life (even when she became a widow) was a gift of love to me. Another gift she gave me—though I chafed under it while she was giving it to me—was the gift of order and organization of one's work. After I became an adult, I realized what a priceless gift this was.

Hannah's gift to her little son Samuel was a handmade garment she brought him every year. That garment said, in effect: "Mother remembers you when you are absent from her. Every minute I handstitched this garment you were in my thoughts. But not only then. I love you always." Samuel knew he was loved. That knowledge was a gift his mother gave to him, and we can't grow and develop without knowing that at least one person in the world loves us.

The Philippian Christians' love gift to Paul was money to help him meet his expenses. They also sent Epaphroditus, one of their own community, to keep Paul company.

Paul's gifts of love to them, in turn, were prayers on their behalf and letters rich in encouragement, affirmation, and instruction. We all need those who believe in and support us.

To the Christians at Corinth Paul gave yet another gift of love, the gift of stern but loving rebuke for wrongs they were doing, the gift of concerned warning, the gift of discipline. "Wounds from a friend can be trusted," the writer of Proverbs observed (Prov. 27:6).

In what ways have you been blessed over the years with gifts of love from family, friends, and even from those who may not have known that they were blessing you? Recall. Give thanks.

How can I thank you adequately for all the gifts of love you have given me, O God? Thank you especially for those who have helped me in my walk with you.

Day 6   Psalm 142   "And free us from all harm."

Lesson from the Thistlebird

A man one day heard a bird chirping outside his bedroom window. Day after day the chirping continued, and the man began to wonder if he detected frantic sounds in the chirping, but the nest was too high in the tree for him to see anything. Then a friend stopped to visit, and the two decided to investigate and found the bird snared in its nest. They took down the nest and spent 20 minutes carefully disentangling one of the bird's legs which had become twisted in the wool that lined its nest. Freed, it flew away, a bit uncertainly, but it flew.

"That was a thistlebird," the friend said. "Thistlebirds always call out when in distress." "I noticed other birds bringing worms to the nest," the man said. "Exactly," his friend said. "Though they couldn't free the bird, they could keep it alive—and they did."

Martin Rinkhart was like that thistlebird. Undoubtedly he had prayed that his country would be "free from all ills" during all his years of pastoral ministry at Eilenberg, yet he never saw his prayer answered. Instead as the war raged on, the suffering around him only grew worse. But though Rinkhart could not free his people, he did all he could to keep them alive. And when they were dying, he spoke God's word of grace to them. God also saved Rinkhart himself from the most deadly ills of all, hatred and despair. Those long, long years, in addition to caring for his people, Rinkhart wrote seven dramas on the Reformation and 66 hymns, many of them hymns of praise.

Perhaps we have loved ones who are suffering from pain of some kind. We wish we could free them, but we cannot. But we can stand by their sides as Rinkhart did. We can love them and ask God for wisdom to be as helpful as we can be to them.

When our loved ones suffer, we too suffer and we too have needs. Focusing only on the needs and hurts of our loved ones can become deadening. Rinkhart found diversion in writing. We too shall need to find our own ways to care for ourselves.

Give me wisdom in this difficult situation, O loving God.